BEYOND
COTTON

making by hand :

STAMP, PRINT, DYE, AND PAINT

KRISTA FLECKENSTEIN

Published in 2015 by Lucky Spool Media, LLC
www.luckyspool.com
info@luckyspool.com

Text © Krista Fleckenstein
Editor Susanne Woods
Designer Rae Ann Spitzenberger
Illustrations Kari Vojtechovsky

Photographs pages 2-3, 4-5, 6, 8-9, 12-13, 18, 20, 22, 26, 40, 42, 44, 46, 62, 64, 66-68, 70, 71, 80, 84, 86, 91, 98, 102, 104, 108, 111, 112, 118, 122, 125, 126, 136, 138, 142, 145, 159-160 © Holly DeGroot

Cover photograph, inside flap, and pages 10, 16, 33, 78-79, 83, 130 © Krista Fleckenstein

Photographs page 117 © Lauren Hunt

All other photography © Paula Pepin

9 8 7 6 5 4 3 2 1

First Edition
Printed in USA

Library of Congress Cataloging-in-Publication Data available upon request

ISBN 978-1-940655-15-4

LSID0027

CONTENTS

INTRODUCTION

Let's start thinking beyond cotton. What does that mean exactly? When most people start sewing, a big part of the fun is visiting the fabric store and picking out prints. It's amazing how much the market has changed since I started making quilts 12 years ago. Back then, batiks were the most colorful fabric I could find! As more modern fabrics made their way to my local shops and online stores, I built quite a stash of amazing quilting cotton prints.

When I started selling pouches through an etsy shop in 2010, I was using that stash of quilting cottons. I soon realized that I could look online and find someone else making pouches that looked just like mine, simply because they used the same fabrics. And worse, I started to realize that my style was subject to whatever was available from fabric companies at that time. I wanted to work with simple, graphic prints so badly, and at that time they were hard to find.

I had always been creative growing up. One of my favorite classes in high school was printmaking, and in college I minored in art. But as many people do, I pushed aside my love of making art when more grown-up responsibilities took over. Quilting and sewing let me be creative on the side, but I was always a bit in awe of the screen-printed fabrics that were being made by designers such as Lara Cameron (Ink & Spindle), Leslie Keating (Maze & Vale), and Karen Lewis (Blueberry Park). It was something I longed to do, but it seemed like an impossible task to learn.

Then I took a QuiltCon workshop called Block Printing on Fabric with Lizzy House in 2012. That course reawakened in me the joy of printmaking that I had left behind in high school. Later that spring, I started making my first screens and got hooked on printing fabric panels. It wasn't easy, but through a bit of advice, and a lot of trial and error, I learned. And I loved it. I started to sew with leather soon after and began selling the same leather-bottom clutches that I'll teach you to sew in this book.

Making my own unique prints and sewing with materials beyond quilt-shop cottons was a turning point for me, where I felt I could control every aspect of how my work looked. I know I'm not alone in that desire to have a distinct voice. I still get hooked on new fabric lines and add plenty of those commercially printed fabrics to my stash, but I like knowing that I can mix them with my own fabrics too.

These days I'm at my best when I have time for making. I'm happiest when I'm surrounded by fabric, thread, paint, and ink. I want you to get to that place too, thinking and sewing beyond cotton. It's time to get inspired, make your own work, and have an amazing time doing it.

HOW TO USE THIS BOOK

This is not just a pattern book. I'm going to teach you, guide you, and help you troubleshoot problems. This book offers you the templates and instructions to make exactly what you see so that you can learn more easily. But ultimately, I don't want you to make something that looks exactly like what I make. I'll tell you how to do it, and then I'll show you how to change things to show your own voice and style.

You'll find that many of the projects use multiple techniques that I teach in this book. But you can still jump around and substitute materials (for example, using a painted piece of canvas in the leather and fabric clutch instead of a screenprinted design).

My hope is that when you read this book, you get inspired to do your own thing. That you will buy a bolt of canvas and mark it up with your own colors and designs. And that you'll consider using more than just fabric when you sew.

Remember that learning is a process. You are going to screw up. You are going to make stuff that might be technically good, but not your style. And let's be honest — you are going to make some really ugly stuff as you experiment. But then it's going to "click". You'll do something right. You'll get comfortable. Your ink colors will sing. You'll build on it. And before you know it, you'll feel so good about making your own things. I promise.

The sewing projects in this book are definitely beginner-friendly, but they do assume that you have basic knowledge of sewing with a home sewing machine. Start with simple projects, like the block printed tea towels (see page 44), if you are new to sewing, but don't be afraid to learn other techniques!

GATHERING INSPIRATION

There is so much to see in the world around us.

I often lag behind on our family walks through the trails by our house. I'm constantly stopping to take photos of plants, both in bloom and decline, and patterns on the birch trees. I'll come home with photos of rocks, bare sticks on top of snow, and worn patterns on the pavement. When it's time to sit down and sketch ideas for a print, I'll try to find ways to simplify the photos I've taken. I'll break the image down so I see lines instead of branches, circles instead of rocks.

I also like to gather information from things inside my home. Objects I see every day in my studio, a simple spool of thread for instance, can make a fun block. I like to rip out pages of catalogs and magazines and paste bits into my sketchbook. Home decor catalogs from companies such as West Elm and Crate and Barrel often give me insight into what the upcoming trends are.

Other artists can be inspiring too. It's okay to learn from other makers and the work that they do. But it's not okay to copy it. Instead, find the aspects of the artists' work that you love. Could it be their use of color? The scale of their prints? Their line quality? For instance, I love using fabrics by Carolyn Friedlander and Leah Duncan when I make quilts — I like the fine lines and hand-drawn feeling of their artwork. Those are characteristics I want to achieve in my own work.

When I get into a creative rut, I find it very important to simplify my influences. A big part of that is unplugging from blogs, Instagram, and Pinterest. It's easy to get too much inspiration from these places, and it can be overwhelming and a bit stifling. Try turning off your phone for the day. Impose a break from posting *and* reading on Instagram for a week. And, for heaven's sake, don't compare your work to anything you see on Pinterest. Grab your sketchbook instead. It will free up your mind for better ideas.

Speaking of your sketchbook...

SKETCHING AND RECORDING

Drawing can be really intimidating — "drawing" sounds like it has to be perfect to be good. But remember that you don't have to do anything perfectly. So sketch instead. Start by sketching shapes. Doodle. Challenge yourself to fill a page a day, or maybe sketch one thing a day. If you feel stuck, grab whatever is nearby and force yourself to study it, then do a five-minute sketch. If you need even more prompting, consider taking an online class. Lisa Congdon's line drawing class on Creativebug is a good one to start with.

You don't need much in the way of supplies to start sketching out your ideas. You should always carry your sketchbook,

Gathering inspiration

pens, and a glue stick with you. It's also good to document your work. In this book, you'll be experimenting with different dye formulas, thread tensions, and materials. Record all those in your sketchbook pages by pasting in the inspirational photos and resulting prints, as well as sample of your experiments.

SKETCHBOOK

The best sketchbook is the one you have with you. With that said, you'll probably learn that you prefer certain features. It's important to have a sketchbook that is small enough (6″ x 9″) to carry with you. It's also beneficial to have one that is larger (12″ x 16″) so you can try sketching larger repeats. I prefer a spiral-bound book with heavy paper so that ink doesn't seep through.

PENS

My favorites are Sakura Pigma Micron pens. They come in packs with different sized tips. For quick drawing and making patterns, I really like the bold lines of the 08, 1, and Brush tip pens. I add in details with the smaller (005, 01, 02, 03, 05) pens. I have a bad habit of leaving the caps off my pens, and these don't dry out. Something to keep in mind, though, is that they are not very airplane-friendly. The cabin pressure decreases after take off and causes them to leak. This has ruined a lot of my pens.

I also really like Pilot and Kuretake brush pens, which I found on the Jet Pens website. Buy a few different brands and see which you like.

DRAFTING TEMPLATES

Drafting templates can be helpful when you want to draw repeating, consistent shapes. You can pick these up at an office supply store.

DID YOU NOTICE THAT I DON'T HAVE A PENCIL ON THE LIST? I think it can be detrimental to the creative process to draw something in pencil and feel like you can fix it with an eraser. Try to practice drawing the same object over and over again with a pen until you get it right. Save the pencil for when you are further along in the design process.

MAKING FABRIC YOUR OWN

Fabric is so wonderful. No one can deny it. I love it in all colors. I love neutrals. I love thick fabric. And I like thin fabric. But best of all, I love knowing how to manipulate it to become something even greater.

In this section I'll go over four basic methods for making fabric your own: painting, block printing, screen printing, and dyeing.

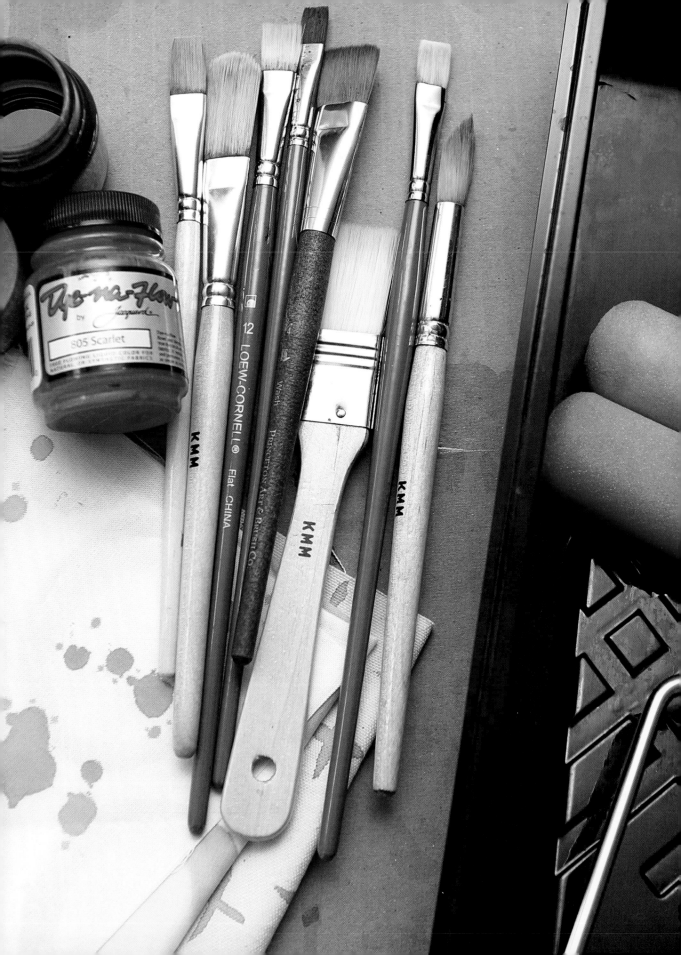

PAINTING FABRIC

My first memories of painting fabric include globs of puffy paint and stiff T-shirts. I think that's why I stayed away from it for as long as I did — it didn't make sense to paint fabric and change the texture so much. But guess what? There is more than puffy paint out there, and painting your own fabric can be a quick and satisfying way to go.

THE TOOLS AND MATERIALS

DYE-NA-FLOW FABRIC DYES

These are little bottles of colorful goodness. Super-saturated, easy-to-mix, and, best of all, they don't change the hand of your fabric! Get a set of basic colors (red, blue, yellow, green, white, etc., that you can mix) but definitely pick out some of the more unusual colors too. Some of my favorites are salmon, hot pink, and turquoise.

FABRIC PAINTS

The paints I've found to have the softest feel on fabric are the Jacquard Textile Paints and Pebeo Setacolor Paints. You can thin them with water for different effects. Jacquard also makes metallic paints in their Lumiere line that are beautiful but can produce a stiffer feel.

HIGH-DENSITY FOAM ROLLERS AND PAINT TRAY

You can get these at the hardware store in the paint section. They are typically used for painting trim and cabinetry, but they make great bold marks on large pieces of fabric.

SYNTHETIC PAINTBRUSHES

Buy a set of flat and round white nylon brushes of all different sizes, and a few larger 1"–2" "utility" paintbrushes.

CONTAINERS FOR MIXING

I use glass mason jars. If you are mixing a large amount of paint or dye, store it in a container with a lid to prevent it from evaporating and getting a "skin." If you do get a skin, pour your dye into another container instead of trying to blend it back in.

EYE DROPPERS

Use these to add small amounts of dye for mixing. You can measure by the drop. I like to use these especially when adding black to tone down a color.

CARDBOARD

Some dyes and paints bleed through, so I place pieces of cardboard from shipping boxes underneath the fabric. The dyes and paints soak just enough into the cardboard without penetrating to a table underneath. It's easy to pin fabric to the cardboard too. If your project is too large, a vinyl-covered tablecloth works well.

MIXING PAINT COLORS

The best way to find your perfect color is to experiment. But here is a chart to show you a few of my favorite formulas for making colors from Dye-Na-Flow.

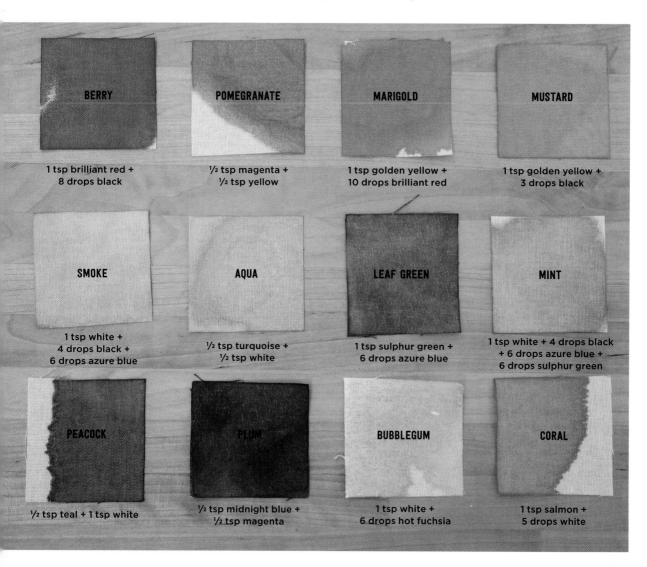

BERRY
1 tsp brilliant red +
8 drops black

POMEGRANATE
½ tsp magenta +
½ tsp yellow

MARIGOLD
1 tsp golden yellow +
10 drops brilliant red

MUSTARD
1 tsp golden yellow +
3 drops black

SMOKE
1 tsp white +
4 drops black +
6 drops azure blue

AQUA
½ tsp turquoise +
½ tsp white

LEAF GREEN
1 tsp sulphur green +
6 drops azure blue

MINT
1 tsp white + 4 drops black
+ 6 drops azure blue +
6 drops sulphur green

PEACOCK
½ tsp teal + 1 tsp white

PLUM
½ tsp midnight blue +
½ tsp magenta

BUBBLEGUM
1 tsp white +
6 drops hot fuchsia

CORAL
1 tsp salmon +
5 drops white

EFFECTS ON DIFFERENT FABRICS

The weave and type of the fabric will affect how your paints and dyes react. A tight-weave fabric such as canvas or sheeting is best for dyes when you want your marks to keep their shape. In a loose-weave fabric like linen, the dye will spread more.

PAINTING ON FABRIC TECHNIQUES

Using a combination of paint straight from the jar and diluted paint can results in a lot of depth. I love transferring ink onto freezer paper first to make sure I like the design and, when I am hapy, I overlay the fabric on top. Each needs different drying times and will require heat setting (see page 20). Try each technique on scrap fabric first.

asy stripes painted in a combination of diluted paint and undiluted paint straight from the jar.

Using wax paper secured to a surface, create a design by dabbing painting or splattering undiluted paint before overlaying your fabric to transfer. Note that the design will be a mirror image when transferred to fabric.

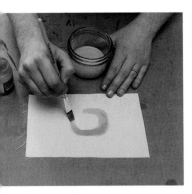 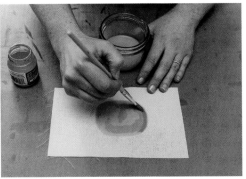 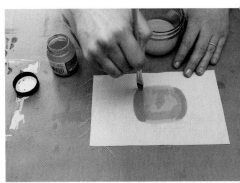

Use this technique for the Baby Bib (see page 18). Create simple shapes and add depth by using a combination of diluted and undiluted paint. Experiment with different widths of brushes to achieve the look you want.

WATERCOLOR
BABY BIB

When my kids were babies, it was such a bummer covering up their cute clothes with the cheesy bibs I could find at the store — so I made my own. I got so much joy out of making my children's bibs, but it's even better making them with fabric you've made! Dye-Na-Flow fabric dyes are perfect for decorating children's items because they soak into the fibers, and don't change the feel of the fabric as paints can. The yardage listed will make one bib

Materials

Bib front fabric: 1 fat quarter (18″ x 22″) white or off-white cotton fabric

Bib backing fabric: 1 fat quarter (18″ x 22″) cotton fleece

1″ piece of ¾″-wide hook and loop tape *or* **1 size 16 metal or plastic snap**

Dye-Na-Flow liquid dyes

Water-soluble pen

PAINTING THE FABRIC

1. Wash, dry, and press your fabric.

2. Referencing the techniques on page 17, lay your piece of cotton on top of your cardboard and paint a fun design **(A)**.

3. Let your fabric dry completely, then heat set with an iron.

> **TIP:** 'Setting' is using heat, usually from an iron, to fix the color permanently to the fabric surface which ensures that the added element is both colorfast and washable. The amount of time for heat setting can vary depending on what paint or dye you are using. For Dye-Na-Flow inks, use the highest setting on your iron that is safe for your base fabric. Keep the hot iron moving over the surface of your fabric for three minutes to properly set the colors.

ASSEMBLING THE BIB

1. Cut (1) 12″ by 18″ piece of both the painted fabric and cotton fleece.

2. Enlarge and trace the bib pattern (see page 147) onto the wrong side of the painted fabric with an erasable marker or pencil **(B)**.

3. Layer the fabrics together, right sides facing (the right side of the fleece in this case is the fuzzy side), with the painted fabric on top **(C)**.

4. Pin the layers together.

5. Using a ¼″ seam allowance, sew the layers together following the traced line, making sure to backstitch at the beginning and end of the marked opening.

6. Trim around the stitch lines, leaving a ¼″ seam allowance. Clip and notch the curves of the bib.

7. Turn the bib right side out, using a blunt object like a chopstick, carefully push out the fabric for a clean shape. Tuck the raw edges of the opening to the inside. Press.

8. Edgestitch ⅛″ around the entire bib, closing up the opening from Step 5 with your stitches in the process **(D)**.

9. Stitch on the hook and loop tape or attach the snap as located on the pattern piece **(E)**.

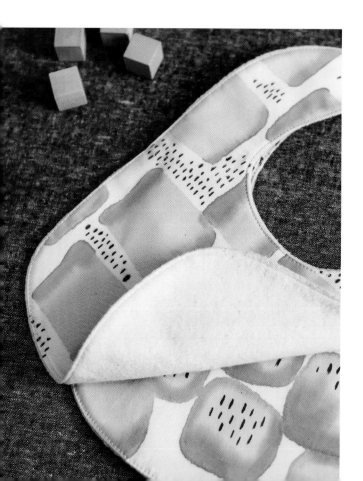

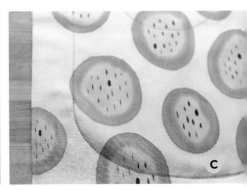

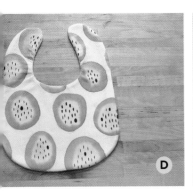

TIP: When making items for babies and young children, always keep safety in mind. I include snaps for decorative reasons, but for practical use, I strongly suggest using hook and loop tape instead. If you do decide to use snaps, test your snaps and fasteners to make sure they are securely fastened to the fabric before you use them. When it comes to secure snaps, try using a Snap Setter. The snaps it comes with are high-quality yet inexpensive, and attach very consistently. I prefer the tool over snap pliers.

Again, snaps are for photo shoots, but please consider using hook and loop tape for baby. Tape releases much more readily if the bib should get caught onto something so are a much safer choice than snaps.

WHOLE CLOTH
PAINTED BABY QUILT

Who says all quilts have to be pieced? You can get graphic and beautiful results by painting a "whole cloth" quilt with dyes and fabric paints. This is my simple version of a landscape, but you can make your own design as easy or as complicated as you like! Try sketching out your design and then colorizing it with watercolors to get an idea of what your dyes will look like. The quilt is finished off in a pillowcase style with ties — no binding or quilting to worry about here!

Finished size:
32" x 40"

Materials

Top fabric: 1 yard white double gauze

Backing fabric: 1 yard

Batting: 45" x 60"

Embroidery floss

Embroidery needle

Dye-Na-Flow dyes in turquoise, white, and sulphur green

Fabric paints in black and white

3-4" Foam paint roller

A piece of cardboard larger than your quilt top *or* **a vinyl tablecloth**

Masking tape and pins

White chalk marker

Water-soluble pen

Acrylic Ruler

Sewing Machine

Coordinating cotton thread

PREPARING THE FABRIC

1. Wash, dry, and press your fabrics.

2. Secure your quilt top fabric to a painting surface **(A)**.

> **TIP:** I prefer using cardboard as a painting surface, but it can be hard to find a piece large enough to do a whole cloth quilt. If you have a large enough piece, smooth your fabric on to the top and secure it with pins. If you can't find a large enough piece of cardboard, use masking tape to secure a vinyl tablecloth to the floor. Smooth the fabric over the top of the vinyl and secure it with masking tape or pins.

PAINTING THE FABRIC

1. Mix your dyes in separate containers **(B)**:

1 tbsp turquoise + 1 tbsp white + ¼ cup water

1 tbsp sulphur green + ¼ cup water

2. Pour the green dye mixture into a shallow pan. Roll the foam paint roller in the dye, saturating the roller **(C)**.

3. Roll the green dye across the lower ⅓ of the quilt, using broad strokes and refilling the roller as needed.

4. Repeat Steps 2 and 3 with the turquoise dye across the top ⅔ of the quilt.

5. Allow the fabric to dry completely.

6. Once the fabric is dry, draw your design on the dyed fabric with a water soluble pen or a white chalk marker (depending on the color of the background) **(D)**.

7. Thin your fabric paint with a little water until it's at the consistency and transparency you prefer.

8. Paint the design with the fabric paint **(E)**. Let dry completely, then heat set with an iron (see page 20).

9. Wash your quilt top in synthrapol to remove any extra paints and dyes. Dry and press.

ASSEMBLING THE QUILT

1. Cut your quilt top, backing and batting to measure 33" x 41".

2. Make your quilt sandwich in this order: backing face up, quilt top face down, and batting on top. Match the edges and pin.

3. Sew around the perimeter of the quilt with a ½" seam allowance, leaving a 6" wide opening on the bottom edge **(F)**. Trim the corners.

> **TIP:** Press the seams open as far as possible. This helps the edges lie flat and look more square when the quilt is turned right side out.

4. Position the layers right side out so the batting is sandwiched in between. Tuck in the edges of the opening from Step 3 and hand stitch it closed using a ladder stitch.

> **LADDER STITCHING:** Closing a seam by hand looks flawless when you use a ladder stitch (see page 117).

5. Press seams flat. Stitch ¼" around the entire perimeter of the quilt **(G)**.

6. Using an acrylic ruler and a water-soluble pen, mark a grid using 4" intervals across the quilt top **(H)**.

7. Use embroidery thread to tie the quilt at each intersection. To do this, thread an embroidery needle with floss. Insert the needle down through all three layers at the mark and then back up again, about

¼" from the entry point. Trim the floss so there is a 2" tail on either side **(I)**. Tie it with a double knot and trim the floss to 1". Repeat on all marks on the grid.

FRECKLES PAINTED TOTE BAG
WITH LEATHER HANDLES

Who doesn't need another tote, especially when it's this cool? It's the details like the boxed bottom, leather straps, and graphic paint technique that make this a stand-out project. This tote is the perfect size for library books or projects on the go. And don't forget: you will easily change the look of the bag by using the fabrics that you have made yourself. Maybe try a dyed canvas for your second version — because, trust me, you can't make just one of these bags.

Materials

Cotton canvas: ½ yard

Lining fabric: ½ yard

Fusible woven interfacing: 1 yard

Leather straps: (2) ¾" x 27" straps in a 3–5 oz. leather

(8) medium metal rivets

Dye-Na-Flow fabric dye in black

3.5mm leather punch

Rivet setter

½" Paint brush

Disappearing ink pen

Cutting

From cotton canvas, cut:
(1) 15" x 32" rectangle

From lining fabric, cut:
(2) 15" x 16½" rectangles

From interfacing, cut:
(1) 15" x 32" rectangle

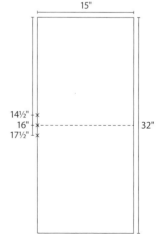

Figure 1

PAINTING THE CANVAS

1. Using a $1/2''$ brush and the Dye-Na-Flow, paint short brush strokes across your piece of canvas **(A)**.

2. Let the dye dry completely, then heat set with an iron (see page 20).

ASSEMBLING THE TOTE

1. Iron the interfacing to the wrong side of the painted canvas.

2. Referencing Figure 1 (see page 27), locate the midpoint of the canvas piece by folding it in half. Mark both sides on the right side of the canvas with a disappearing ink pen. Place additional marks $1 1/2''$ from the midpoint on each side for a total of 6 transferred marks **(B)**.

3. Fold the midpoint marks so they meet up with one set of marks, right sides together. Pin in place **(C)**.

4. Repeat on the other side. The midpoint will now be sandwiched between two layers of canvas, with right sides together, and the short ends of the canvas will align.

5. Stitch along both sides of the canvas using a $3/8''$ seam allowance and backstitching at both ends. Press.

6. Place the two lining pieces right sides together and sew along the bottom raw edges using a $1/2''$ seam allowance, making sure to leave a 6" opening in the center for turning **(D)**.

7. Repeat Steps 2–5 with the lining fabric.

8. Turn the outer canvas part of the bag right side out. Place it inside the lining with right sides together, match up the top edges and pin **(E)**.

9. Sew the two layers together along the top raw edge using a $1/2''$ seam allowance.

10. Pull the bag right side out through the opening in the lining. Tuck the lining inside the outer bag and press the top edge where they meet. Topstitch **(F)**.

11. Stitch the opening closed using a ladder stitch (see page 117).

ATTACHING THE LEATHER HANDLES

1. Prepare your leather handles by punching 2 holes $1/2''$ and $1 1/4''$ from the end of each strap with a 3.5 mm punch **(G)**.

> **TIP:** I make sure that the holes match by punching both holes on one strap end first, then using it as a template of sorts to mark the other strap ends.

2. Place a strap $3 1/2''$ from each side of the bag. The end of the strap will overlap the bag by $1 3/4''$. Mark the bag through the holes of the strap **(H)**.

3. Remove the strap and punch holes through the layers of the bag using the 3.5 mm punch.

4. Realign and attach the leather straps with a rivet in each hole, making sure that each strap is not twisted **(I)**.

BUILDING A PADDED PRINTING SURFACE

Textile printing requires a surface with a bit of cushion. Starting out, my first padded printing surface was a Hawaiian beach towel taped to a piece of masonite. It worked, but it was hard to get a consistent print. Since then, I've developed this simple portable printing surface. It will save you loads of trouble and ensure that you can print anywhere with a stable surface. The materials are inexpensive and easy to find.

Materials

24" x 48" wood panel (a tabletop or level piece of plywood)

2¾ yards of 36"-wide wool-blend felt

45" x 60" thin cotton batting (1 crib-size package)

Canvas drop cloth

Temporary spray adhesive

Staple gun and staples

(12) 2⅛" round self-adhesive furniture glides

(12) 1½" round self-adhesive, anti-skid furniture pads

SURFACE SIZE: 24" x 48" is the surface size that works for me in my studio. But it's easy to customize! Ask your local hardware store to cut your piece of wood panel to the exact size you need, and adjust your materials to fit!

Cutting

From felt, cut:
(2) 24" x 48" rectangles

From batting, cut:
(1) 26" x 50" rectangle

From canvas, cut:
(2) 30" x 54" rectangles

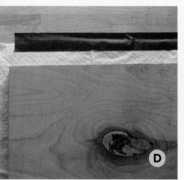

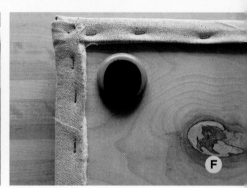

ASSEMBLY

1. Gather together your materials **(A)**.

2. Lay your wood panel faceup. Place a felt rectangle on top of the wood panel, matching the edges. Fold back half of the felt and apply the spray adhesive on the exposed wood panel. Smooth the felt over the adhesive, repositioning and smoothing as necessary to make sure there are no bumps **(B, C)**.

3. Fold the remaining half of the felt back and repeat Step 2.

4. Layer the second felt rectangle on top of the first layer and repeat Steps 2–3.

5. Lay your batting on a clean surface, smoothing out any large wrinkles. It helps to tape it down with a few pieces of masking tape or painter's tape to keep the batting flat **(D)**.

6. Place the wood panel felt side down and centered on the batting. Wrap the batting around the wood panel, pulling it smooth and tight. Attach it to the back using a staple gun **(E)**.

7. Repeat Step 6 with the 2 pieces of canvas. Attaching each canvas layer individually lets you replace the top layer of canvas after it gets covered in ink.

8. Apply the furniture glides to the bottom of the wood panel (one in each corner and the rest spread evenly along the edges and center). Adhere an anti-skid pad on the center of each glide **(F)**.

BLOCK PRINTING

Block printing is one of the easiest ways to get a consistent pattern transferred onto fabric. Here, I will teach you how to create your own blocks. Once you master the basics, I encourage you to make them as simple or as elaborate as you like.

THE BASICS

RUBBER CARVING MATERIAL

There are a great many types available, so I encourage you to experiment with a few to find your own personal preference. To get you started, here are some of my favorites:

Moo Carve: This is a soft, easy-to-carve material that holds ink really nicely. The downside is it's a bit fragile. You have to take a lot of care when handling and cleaning the blocks made from Moo Carve or they can tear.

Soft-Kut: This is also very soft and easy to carve. It's thinner tha Moo Carve, about ¼" thick, and benefits from being mounted on a piece of plexiglass.

Speedball Speedy-Carve: This pink material is a bit more firm and holds detail well without tearing.

PLEXIGLASS

Plexiglass is used for mounting blocks. While not necessary, it does help to stabilize more delicate designs and keeps your fingers clean. You can mount to wood blocks too, but the plexi allows you to easily see where you're stamping. Get a ¼"-thick sheet at your local hardware store, score it with a plastic cutting knife, and sand any sharp edges.

STRONG GLUE

You will need a strong glue such as Super Glue™ for attaching your carved blocks to the plexiglass.

LINOLEUM CUTTERS

A set of lino cutters is inexpensive and does all you need! Speedball and Dick Blick both make good ones. Replacement blades are available when yours get dull. A lino cutter set comes with five different blades:

Small V (1) : Great for cutting out detail. Use this to go around the edge of your design first.

Large V (2): Good for cleaning out tight areas, doing thick line work.

Small U Gouge (3): Good for scooping out interior areas of negative space.

Large U Gouge (4): Ideal for carving out large areas of negative space.

Knife (5): Suitable for slicing away pieces.

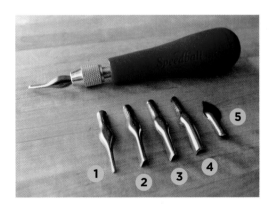

X-ACTO KNIFE

I like using this tool for cutting away the excess rubber material from the outside of the design.

PENCIL AND VELLUM OR TRACING PAPER

You'll need these to trace and transfer designs to your rubber material. Be sure not to use a colored pencil as they do not contain any graphite, the presence of which is essential to the transfer process.

INKS

VersaCraft ink pad: This is one of my favorite, readily available stamp pads. It is permanent when used on fabric, and it comes in a good range of colors.

Screen printing fabric inks: The benefit of using screen printing inks and making your own stamp pads for block printing is that you aren't limited to certain colors, as you are when using a store-bought ink pad. My favorite brand is Permaset. I've also used Speedball inks with good results.

MAKING AN INK PAD

Materials

Craft felt (white or off-white is best)

Paper plate

Screen printing ink or fabric paint

Spoon

1. Cut a piece of craft felt at least 1″ larger than your carving block on all sides and place it on a paper plate **(A)**.

2. Drop a spoonful of ink onto the felt and rub it in with the back of your spoon. You want to saturate the felt and avoid having left over ink glops sitting on top of the surface of the felt **(B)**.

3. Press your block into the ink pad a few times until the block surface is covered evenly with ink.

MAKING A BLOCK

Materials

Rubber carving block

X-Acto knife

Pencil

Velum or tracing paper

Lino carving kit

PREPARING THE BLOCK

1. Gather your materials **(A)**.

2. Cut your rubber material slightly bigger than your image using an X-Acto knife.

3. Rub the surface of the rubber block lightly across an ink pad and wipe away the excess ink with a paper towel. This process stains the rubber and makes it easier to see where you are carving.

4. Lay a piece of vellum or tracing paper over your image and trace it with a pencil, making sure to leave a good layer of graphite on the surface **(B)**.

5. Place the traced artwork on top of your rubber material, graphite side down. Holding it steady, rub the back of a spoon (or other smooth object) over the entire area of your traced image, transferring the graphite to the rubber **(C, D)**.

6. Start carving!

BONUS: Use the Project Artwork (see page 146) to practice carving blocks that you can substitute in for the ones in the following projects. Practice repeats and making fabric panels on scrap fabric or muslin until you get the pressure just right. Just follow the instructions above and practice until you get the hang of it.

CARVING THE BLOCK

SAFETY FIRST: Always cut away from your body! Hold the bottom of the block with your hand and carve the lines toward the top. Rotate the block instead of rotating your hand.

1. Set your rubber block on a solid surface. I like to put a piece of paper underneath to catch the rubber shavings and make clean up easier.

2. Begin by using your lino cutter #1 small V blade. Hold the cutter so that it's at a 30-degree angle to your block, apply light pressure, and carve the details of your stamp **(E)**. Make sure that the top edges of the blade do not go beneath the surface of the rubber, or it will tear the block **(F)**.

3. Periodically brush away stray shavings with your hand or a small paintbrush **(G)**.

4. Cut away the outer edges of your block using an X-Acto knife always keeping your fingers away from the line of cutting **(H)**.

5. Switch to one of your U gouge (small #3 or large #5 depending on the size of the area) and begin to carve away the negative space. Make sure you are also carving away the little ridge lines that appear in large areas of negative space.

6. If preferred, mount your block onto a piece of plexiglass (see page 33) with a dab of strong glue and set aside to allow the glue to dry.

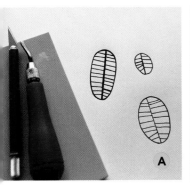

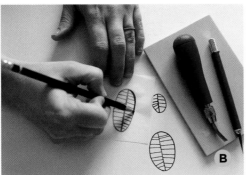

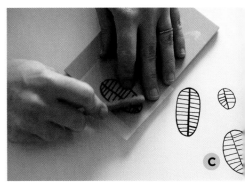

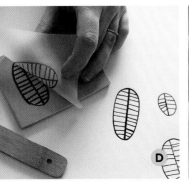

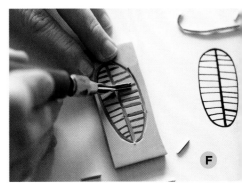

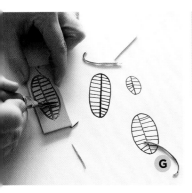

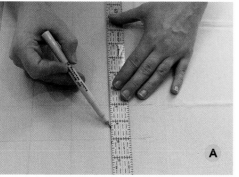

TESTING THE BLOCK PRINT

Before you start printing on your prepared fabric, always do a test print. I do an initial print on paper, but then I always grab a scrap of fabric to test on too. The print can look different on different surfaces. If necessary, use your lino cutter to remove more stamping material to get it to look the way you want it.

PRINTING

1. Place your fabric on your printing surface. If your fabric is thin and you are worried about ink seeping through, place a thicker piece of scrap fabric underneath.

2. Mark your fabric if you want to create a repeating pattern and aren't comfortable just eyeballing it. One of my favorite marking methods is to create a grid of creases using my iron. You can also mark your pattern placement with chalk or a disappearing ink pen **(A)**.

3. Press your carved block into your ink pad repeatedly to cover the surface with a thick layer of ink. Take care not to get any ink on your fingers during this step! You don't want to unintentionally transfer any unwanted ink onto your fabric **(B)**.

4. Place your block over the fabric and press it into the fibers. You want to apply even pressure, but it doesn't have to be extreme. You can use your fingers or the palm of your hand.

5. Lift your block straight up off the surface and admire your work **(C)**!

> **TIP:** Does your print look blurry? First, make sure your ink pad does not have big globs of ink on it, and then make sure that the carved lines on your block are cut deeply enough into the surface.

> **HEAT SETTING:** After the ink has dried completely, you need to heat set it to make sure it won't wash out of the fabric. Iron your fabric on high heat for three or four minutes, keeping your iron moving so you don't scorch your design. If you are doing multiple items (for example, panels of fabric or towels), place your items in a clothes dryer and dry on high heat for one hour.

ADDITIONAL BLOCK PRINTING ARTWORK IDEAS

SUPER HASHTAG
BLOCK PRINTED SCARF

A carved block print doesn't have to use complicated designs. Sometimes the simplest designs make the biggest impact! The block used for this scarf takes just a few minutes to prepare and carve. It can be layered and repeated in so many different ways, but for this project, I like it overlapped in a bit of a super hashtag style. Pair a bold ink with a silky chambray fabric and you can transform this project into a bulkier cozy scarf. You can't lose! Hashtag? #awesome

Materials

Light fabric: ½ yard of shot cotton, chambray, or crossweave in a light tint or hue

Dark fabric: ½ yard of shot cotton, chambray, or crossweave in a dark shade or hue

Coordinating thread

Rubber carving material

Screen printing ink

Cutting

From the light fabric and dark fabric, cut:
(1) 17″ x WOF rectangle from each

CARVING

1. Trace the # template (see page 146) and transfer it to your rubber block. Carve out the channels with your lino cutter #2 large V blades. Trim the edges. If desired, mount your stamp onto plexiglass.

2. If you'd like to use your own hashtag design, cut a rectangle that has a 2:1 length to width ratio (for example, 2" long x 1" wide, 3" long x 1½" wide, etc.) and carve out even vertical channels with your lino cutter #2 large V blade.

PRINTING

1. Place the lighter fabric on your printing surface. If you want a regular pattern, mark your fabric with a water-soluble pen accordingly. For my scarf, I chose to eyeball a half-drop repeat and used my hand to estimate spacing.

2. Prepare an ink pad and test your block print on scrap fabric first **(A)**.

3. Press the block on your fabric once **(B)**, then reload with ink and press again on top of the previous mark to form the "+" design **(C, D)**.

4. Continue to print across your fabric. If your print pattern extends off the fabric, slip a piece of paper underneath the edge to catch the extra ink so you can keep your work area free of ink **(E, F)**.

5. Let the ink air dry (it can take anywhere from fifteen to thirty minutes), then heat set with an iron (see page 20).

SEWING

1. Place your fabrics right sides together, matching up the selvedge edges. Sew each short side together using a ³⁄₈" seam allowance. Press the seams open **(G)**. You'll end up with a big tube of fabric.

2. Press both long sides of the scarf tube ¼" to the wrong side, then ¼" again to enclose the raw edge. Sew **(H)**. Topstitch ⅛" away from both sides of the seam from Step 1 to secure the selvedge edges.

TIP: The length of this scarf allows you to wrap it around your neck twice for a looser look, or three times for a cozy feel.

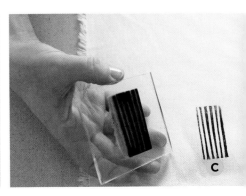

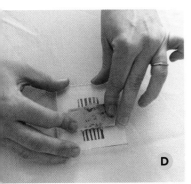

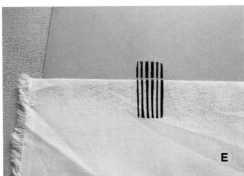

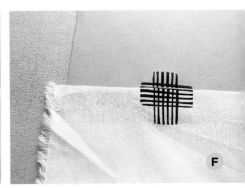

SPRING FIELD
BLOCK PRINTED TEA TOWEL

Who doesn't need an extra set of tea towels? In this project, you'll carve three separate blocks that will work together to make a design along the edge of the towels. You can use the blocks separately on other projects later. The yardage listed in the Materials list will make two large tea towels.

Finished Size:
18" x 28"

Materials

Linen/cotton blend fabric: 1 yard

6" of ½"-wide twill tape

(2) 4" x 6" rubber carving blocks

Screen printing ink and ink pad (see page 34)

Disappearing ink pen or tailor's chalk

Cutting

From your fabric, cut:
(2) 20" x 30" panels

From your twill tape, cut:
(2) 3" pieces

TIP: Before cutting, pre-wash your fabric, dry, and press. This is because this type of fabric has a particularly high shrinkage rate and the towels will be washed often.

CARVING

1. Trace the templates (see page 146) and transfer them to your rubber block. The group of three flowers will fit on one block, and the sets of two flowers will each fit on the other blocks.

2. Carve your stamps, first outlining the detail with the lino cutter #1 small V blade, then cleaning up the designs with the larger blades.

3. Mount your stamps to individual pieces of plexiglass if preferred.

PRINTING

1. Gather your materials **(A)**.

2. Position the fabric so a short edge is on your printing surface.

3. Mark a line 1″ away from the raw edge of the fabric with chalk or a disappearing ink pen.

4. Prepare an ink pad and test your blocks on scrap fabric before continuing **(B)**.

5. Using the mark from Step 3 as a guide, print across the bottom of the towel, lining up the bottom of the blocks with your marked line **(C)**. Alternate the three blocks as you go **(D)**.

6. Place a piece of paper under the edges of your fabric to print off the side and catch any extra ink.

7. Repeat Steps 4 and 5 on the opposite short side of the towel.

8. Let the ink air dry (it can take anywhere from fifteen to thirty minutes), then heat set with an iron (see page 20) **(E)**.

SEWING

1. Press the long edges of each side of one towel ¼″ wrong sides together. Press under ¼″ again to enclose the raw edge **(F)**.

2. Topstitch the hems **(G)**.

3. Repeat Step 1 along both short sides.

4. Fold one piece of twill tape in half to form a loop. Tuck the raw edges under one unsewn hem on the short side positioning the tape, 1″ away from the long edge. Pin **(H)**.

5. Topstitch along the two short hems **(I)**.

6. Repeat to complete the second towel.

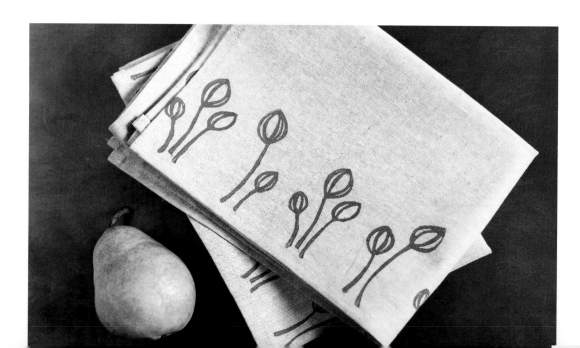

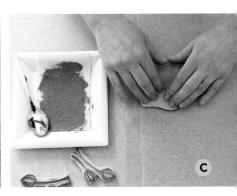

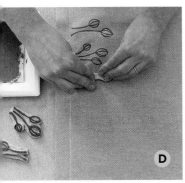

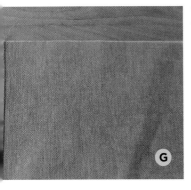

SCREEN PRINTING

When I became interested in screen printing, I had absolutely no idea where to begin. I received a basic Speedball kit for Christmas and pored through the instructions, but I quickly realized there weren't many guidelines for printing onto textiles. So I winged it and got frustrated by producing bad prints, not to mention all that wasted fabric. It took a lot of trial and error and advice from friends before I figured out what worked well. Screen printing is a fun way to produce the unique fabric you've always dreamed of — just remember that the learning process can be just as exciting as seeing the results!

My goal is to get you successfully started at screen printing without the headaches that I experienced. The first step to ensure this doesn't happen, is for you to gather the right supplies. This will save you a lot of time and will give you consistent finished results. The selection of supplies can be daunting, so here is my guide to all of the essentials you will need to get started.

THE BASICS

SCREENS
I like aluminum frame screens from Blick Art. A versatile size to start with for every project in this book is 20" x 24". This size often fits in a kitchen sink for cleaning. They dry quickly and they don't warp. Basic 110 mesh is just fine for printing on fabric.

TIP: Keep in mind that your design ideally should have at least 2" of space from the raw edges of both sides and the bottom, and at least 3" at the top.

DRAWING FLUID AND SCREEN FILLER
Use these to draw a design directly on the screen.

ADHESIVE STENCIL VINYL, MASK-EASE, TRACING PAPER
These materials are used for creating a printing stencil. If you use a cutting machine, you'll need rolls of adhesive vinyl.

X-ACTO KNIFE
This is an indispensable tool for cutting out stencils and for a variety of other tasks too.

PHOTO EMULSION

Begin with Speedball or Ulano brand diazo emulsions. These have given me consistent results and are easy to find at your local art supply store or online.

INKS

Use water-based inks for easy clean-up and less toxicity. I started with Speedball inks but now mostly use Permaset inks. There are a ton of pre-mixed colors, or you can mix your own with basic white, black, magenta, cyan and yellow inks.

SQUEEGEES

Please buy yourself a good squeegee! Sure, those plastic ones work (and you can even go as basic as using a credit card for smaller prints) — but your results will be more consistent, and your wrists much happier, if you buy a rubber squeegee with an aluminum or wood handle. Aluminum dries faster, but I prefer the feel of wood. I recommend using a 60–65 durometer squeegee. The size of the squeegee should be 2″ smaller than your screen width. For example, use a 16″ squeegee with an 18″ wide screen.

PLASTIC SPREADER

This is my favorite tool for cleaning extra ink off screens and squeegees.

INK STORAGE

When you mix your own colors, you will need to store them in airtight containers. I like the round plastic ware bowls with screw-on lids because they are less likely to spill. But you can reuse old sour cream containers, mason jars, etc. Just be careful with glass containers in areas with hard floors (ask me how I know).

PLASTIC OR METAL SPOONS AND RUBBER SPATULAS

You'll use these for mixing inks and applying them to your screen. The best place to get these is the thrift shop.

PAINTERS TAPE AND PACKING TAPE

Use these for taping off the edges of the screen and marking your printing surface.

INKJET TRANSPARENCIES

You can use these to print out positive images from your computer to use with photo emulsion.

INDIA INK AND OPAQUE PAINT MARKERS

Opaque inks are used for drawing positives directly on a transparency for photo emulsion. Use India Ink with a brush or an opaque paint marker such as Sakura Pen-touch in black.

> **TIP:** Always do a test print on scrap fabric or muslin before you start printing on your "good" fabric. I use an old piece of fabric that's been printed over many times.

SCREEN PRINTING TECHNIQUES

Materials

Padded printing surface (see page 30)

Prepared screen

Inks

Spoons (plastic or metal) for scooping ink

Squeegee

Plastic spreader

Masking tape

Prepared fabric

TIP: I use an old jelly roll pan to corral my ink, squeegee, plastic spreader, spoon, and tape in one place. It's also important to have all your fabric cut, pressed, and ready to go.

MARKING THE PRINTING SURFACE

To ensure consistent printing, mark your padded surface with masking tape.

First, mark the corners where the screen will lay. Place a piece of fabric under the screen and work to get it centered under your design. When you have it just right, take the screen off and mark the corners around the fabric too **(A)**.

LET'S PRINT!

1. Before you print, apply masking tape along each inside edge of the screen to keep the ink from seeping out. This makes cleanup easier too **(B)**.

2. Place the fabric on your surface within the masking tape marks and position the screen bottom side down on top of your fabric **(C)**.

3. Spread a generous amount of ink across the top of your screen with a spoon (in the area above the design). The line of ink should be as wide as your squeegee **(D)**.

4. Grab your squeegee firmly with both hands and place it in the ink at a 45-degree angle. Wiggle it around to get it loaded up with ink **(E)**.

5. Pull your squeegee down the screen, keeping even pressure. You don't want to feel a lot of drag on the screen, but it shouldn't feel like your squeegee is floating **(F)**.

6. Because fabric is more absorbent than paper, I find that a second pass of ink is needed for a nice and dark print. With your squeegee still at the bottom of the screen, pick it up and wiggle it into your pool of ink at the bottom of the screen, roll your hands forward so the 45-degree angle faces away from you, and do a push of ink to the top **(G)**.

7. Rest the handle of your squeegee against the top of the screen frame. Lift the bottom of your screen while the top edge remains on your surface. The fabric will stick to the screen, so hold on to a clean corner and pull down as you lift the screen **(H)**.

8. Place a large container of ink underneath the bottom of the screen to hold it up and slowly pull your fabric out from underneath to keep it from folding on itself **(I)**.

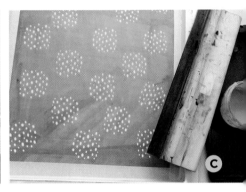

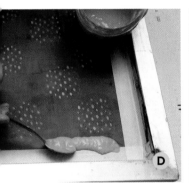

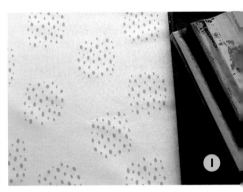

9. Lay your fabric flat on a table or drape it across the back of a chair, whatever you have! I use a clothes-drying rack when I do multiple panels.

10. Let the ink dry completely. This can take anywhere from 10 minutes to longer than an hour depending on humidity. Heat set it with an iron (see page 20).

CLEANING UP

After you're done printing, scrape off extra ink from the screen and squeegee with the plastic spreader and put it back into the ink container before you clear your screen. Then, spray your screen and other equipment with cool water. Use your hands and a soft toothbrush to wash away any remaining ink. Dry everything immediately to prevent warping.

MAKING THE SCREEN

STENCIL METHOD

Screen printing with a vinyl or paper stencil is one of the easiest ways to start, because you don't need to invest in chemicals. You simply create a stencil that the ink can pass through. This works best with simple designs that don't have a lot of small areas of unprinted negative space.

Which stencil material is best? It depends. Tracing paper is inexpensive, easy to apply, and easy to cut, but it can be used only for a single print run since you can't rinse the ink off. Vinyl is more expensive, trickier to apply, and a little harder to cut, but it can be used for multiple print runs.

1. Trace the mirror image of your design onto your paper or vinyl. Remember that the areas you will cut away will be the areas that print onto your fabric. Sometimes it can be helpful to mark the areas you'll cut away with an X **(A)**.

2. Place the stencil material on top of a cutting mat and use an X-Acto knife to trim away the positive areas of your design **(B)**.

3. If you are using Mask-Ease, you will place a piece of transfer paper on top of your cutout design. This helps keep your stencil in good shape as it's being stuck to the screen.

4. Adhere your stencil to the screen using one of the following two methods:

Paper: If you are using paper as your stencil material, center the stencil right side down on the bottom of your screen (the side that will lay directly on your fabric). Tape down all sides with masking tape (this makes it easier to reposition without hurting your stencil) **(C)**.

Vinyl: If you are using vinyl as your stencil material, carefully peel off the paper backing and mount it to the bottom of your screen (the side that will lay directly on your fabric) by attaching one edge, slowly pulling off the protective paper, and pressing it down against the mesh with a squeegee **(D)**.

5. Tape off the remaining open screen with packing tape to prevent ink from leaking around your stencil **(E)**.

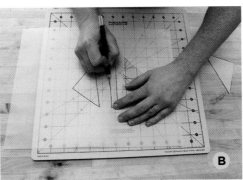

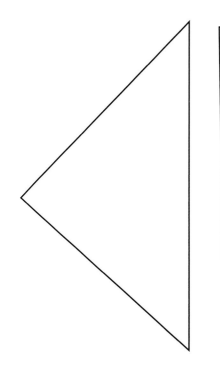

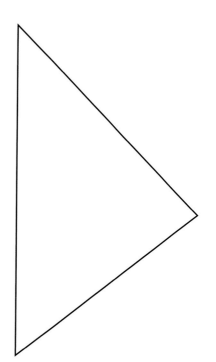

DRAWING FLUID METHOD

Drawing fluid is another great tool for making screens. A water-soluble blue liquid, it is painted directly onto the screen to make the design you wish to print. It's an easy process, but it can be time consuming if you are creating a complicated design, so I like to use this method for projects that feature clean lines and simple shapes.

1. Using a permanent marker, trace your image onto a piece of wax paper or the shiny side of freezer paper exactly as you want it to print.

2. Lay the wax paper face down onto the bottom of the screen (the side that will lay directly on your fabric). Secure it with a couple of pieces of masking tape to keep it from slipping around. Flip your screen over onto a flat surface. The open frame will be facing you and you will see your design easily through the mesh.

3. Dip a round, stiff paintbrush just into the surface of the drawing fluid. Run it along the top edge of the container to get off any extra fluid.

4. Begin painting directly on top of the screen, following the lines you drew on the wax paper. Use short strokes and refill your brush regularly. To keep a steadier hand, brace you arm on the edges of the screen **(A, B)**.

5. When your design is fully dry (test for tacky areas after one hour), peel off the wax paper and check to see if any areas need more drawing fluid added on the bottom side. It doesn't have to be a thick layer, but you want to make sure there are no visible holes. You can check this by holding it up to a light or a window. Let any repairs fully dry again.

6. Lay out a sheet of newspaper to protect your table and place your screen on top, this time with the bottom side of the screen facing up.

7. Pour a line of screen filler across one end of the screen **(C)** and quickly pull it down with a squeegee over the design to fill the screen **(D)**. **It's very important to do this in a single pass.** Because the screen filler has moisture in it, it begins to dissolve the drawing fluid. If you do a second pass, it disturbs the design and ruins the screen. Wipe off any extra screen filler from your pull and let dry.

8. Take your screen to your washing area and run cold water over it. The drawing fluid will begin to dissolve. You can help it dissolve by rubbing it gently with a brush, but don't scrub it **(E)**.

9. Let your screen dry, then hold it up to a light or window to check for any holes in your screen filler. You can paint the screen filler directly on the screen to fix them **(F)**.

10. Before you print, cure your screen by placing it in a sunny window for a couple of hours, or give it a 10-minute blast from a halogen work light. Don't skip this step, or you might damage the screen filler **(G)**.

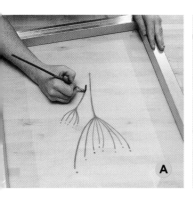

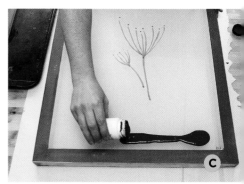

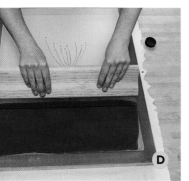

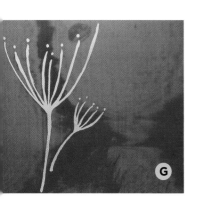

PHOTO EMULSION METHOD

In this method, you start by coating a screen with a photosensitive chemical emulsion. You create an opaque design on a transparency sheet that essentially blocks areas of the screen from being exposed to light. The emulsion hardens after the light exposure and creates a permanent stencil on the screen.

Materials

Lamp with yellow bug light bulb

Screen

Emulsion

Squeegee

Image positive

Exposure unit

COATING THE SCREEN

1. Diazo emulsions (Speedball, Ulano) require mixing a small bottle of chemicals with the emulsion before you can apply it to your screen. Follow the instructions that come with your emulsion.

2. Turn on your lamp with the bug light bulb and turn off any other sources of light in the room. Cover your work surface with paper to protect it.

3. Place your screen top down on the table. Pour a line of emulsion along one edge **(A)** and pull it across with your squeegee to coat the mesh. Unlike using the drawing fluid method (see page 56), it's okay to make multiple passes using this process **(B)**. Flip your screen over and spread out any drips that come through on the top of the screen.

4. Let the emulsion dry in a completely dark place with the screen lying flat. This could take a few hours or a couple days depending on the humidity. If you do not have a dark room, line a shallow box (big enough for your screen) with black duct tape and place the screen inside.

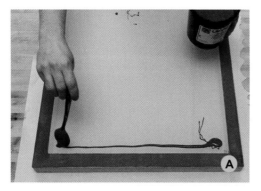

PREPARING POSITIVES

There are a few different ways to make what is called a "positive" for printing:

1. You can draw your design directly onto transparencies or acetate with india ink or black acrylic paint pens.

2. You can use objects to block light by placing them directly on the screen (think scattered pennies to make large dots).

3. You can print images from your computer onto inkjet transparencies using your home printer.

I like to draw or stamp a design, scan it into a design program like Photoshop to clean it up, and then play around with layouts. Then, I either print an arranged design directly onto the transparencies or print multiple images that I cut out and arrange directly on top of the screen.

EXPOSING THE SCREEN

There are so many ways to go about exposing your screen for printing. Play with a few different methods to experiment with the results. Before you try any of these methods, it is important that you screen is completely dry.

Use the sun: If you live in a location that has consistent sunlight, you can use the sun to expose your screen. Try and do this when the sun is at it's highest point in the sky so that you get even exposure.

REMEMBER: Because photo emulsion is light-sensitive, all steps of burning a screen, need to done in a dark room lit only with a yellow incandescent bug light (this light won't react with the emulsion). If you have a room without windows, you can do this any time. But if you don't, you will need to wait until night to burn your screens. (You can imagine that causes a bit of an issue for me during Alaskan summers!)

Purchase a professional exposure unit: If consistent sunlight isn't achievable for you, professional units can be purchased through online retailers like Dharma Trading and EBay. They can range anywhere from $79 to over $2000. Follow the instructions that come with your specific unit.

Build your own exposure unit: There are multiple tutorials online for building your own exposure unit, from modifying a basic halogen work light to building a glass-covered table with UV black light bulbs. Because consistent sunlight is a challenge during Alaskan winters, I've modified my own halogen light to create an exposure unit and have had great success.

Rent time at a screen printing studio: As screen printing becomes more popular, local art centers and screen printing shops will rent time on their equipment. Check and see if you have one available in your area!

Hire it out: Do you have a local screen printing shop that prints things like t-shirts? They likely have their own equipment for making custom screens for their jobs, and might be willing to make a screen for you. There are online services that will burn screens and send them to you in the mail. The benefit of doing this is that you won't need to invest in screen frames and emulsions. The downside is that it can be expensive, and you don't have the instant gratification of when you do it yourself.

Preparing for exposure: No matter what method you use, you need to have a few things ready to go to set up your screen for exposure. These techniques can be used with sun exposure or an exposure unit that uses overhead lighting. If you use a professional unit, follow their provided instructions.

SETTING UP AN EXPOSURE AREA

I set up my exposure area in my studio. I hang the light off the end of my desk, and place either my sewing machine or one of my husband's weights on top of the wood to keep it steady.

Materials

Non-UV ¼" glass that measures the same size as your screen opening

A piece of black felt bigger than your screen

A piece of 2-inch-thick foam, cut just smaller than the inside of your screen

Exposure unit

Lamp with a yellow bug light bulb

TIP: Don't forget to do each of these steps while the room is dark and you are using only a yellow bug light!

1. Gather your materials **(A)**.

2. Stuff the piece of foam inside the top of your screen so it sits flush against the mesh **(B)**.

3. Place the screen bottom side up on the surface you are using for exposure.

4. Place your positive transparency facedown on the screen and center it.

5. Place the glass on top of the transparency. This keeps the transparency flat and steady during the exposure **(C)**.

6. Turn on your exposure unit. Depending on the light source and your emulsion, it can take anywhere from three (on a sunny summer afternoon) to 13 minutes (for a homemade setup using a halogen light). If you have trouble getting the exposure time correct, you can purchase an exposure calculator online to help determine the right amount of time. **(D)**.

RINSING THE SCREEN

1. When the time is up, carefully remove the hot glass and foam from the screen and take the screen to your sink.

2. Use the sprayer to blast cool water onto your screen. If your emulsion developed properly, you will start to see your image come through as the unexposed emulsion washes away. You can lightly rub the image with your fingers or a soft toothbrush to encourage the emulsion to wash away **(E)**.

3. Once your image is completely clear, let your screen dry, then hold it up to a light or window to check for any holes. Paint screen filler directly on the screen to fix them as you did in Step 9 in the Drawing Fluid Method (see page 56).

4. Before you print again, cure your screen by placing it in a sunny window for a couple hours, or give it another 10-minute blast from the exposure unit.

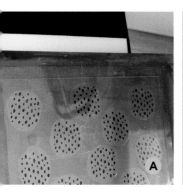

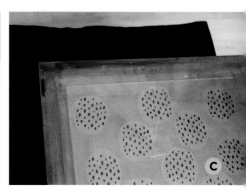

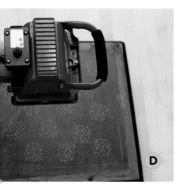

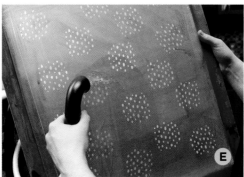

BONUS: You can create unique screen-printed fabric panels by using any of the artwork in this book but I encourage you to create your own designs—that's half the fun! Trace and cut out a vinyl or paper stencil, trace your chosen design with drawing fluid, or scan a design and make a positive for printing with emulsion. The possibilities are endless!

NATURE'S ABSTRACT
CANVAS ARTWORK

Going for an abstract or improv look is a good way to layer prints and colors without worrying about perfection. By using stencils, you can make one-of-a-kind designs with just a single screen. Play with colors and placement as you work. The design I used should just be a guideline — there is really no wrong way to create this no-sew beginner project!

Materials

Fabric: linen or canvas, cut to 16" x 20"

(1) 12" x 16" artist-wrapped canvas, 1" deep

(1) 20" x 24" screen

(1) 12" x 48" roll of white adhesive vinyl

Squeegee

Cutting Mat

X-Acto knife

Masking tape

Packing tape

Screen printing ink in 3 colors (black, mustard, leaf green)

Staples and staple gun

PREPARING THE STENCILS

1. Trace your design (see pages 148-150) on to the non-adhesive side of 3 separate pieces of vinyl (1 per color). To make lining them up easier for printing, stack each piece of tracing paper on top of the previous one as you trace **(A)**.

2. Tape to a cutting mat to secure the vinyl. One sheet at a time, cut out the designs with a X-Acto knife **(B)**.

ATTACHING

1. Place the first vinyl stencil face down on the bottom of the screen so that it is 6″ from the top outside edge of the screen and 5″ from the left side **(C)**. Use your squeegee to ensure a wrinkle-free bond **(D)**. Tape the edges down with masking tape.

2. Fill in the remainder of the bottom of the screen with packing tape **(E)**.

PRINTING

1. Center your piece of fabric under the design on the screen. Mark the screen position on your printing surface with tape **(F)**.

2. Print the first design. Leave it on the printing surface **(G)**.

3. Remove any extra ink from the screen, then remove the tape and stencil. Rinse the screen thoroughly (see page 60) and let it dry.

4. Repeat Steps 1–3 for mounting the screen with your second and third vinyl stencils, using the same masking tape marks on the printing surface to accurately position your screen.

5. Let the final artwork dry, then heat set with a hot iron (see page 20) for 3–4 minutes, keeping your iron moving so you don't scorch your design.

MOUNTING

1. Place the artwork face down, and center the artist canvas face down on top of that **(H)**.

2. Pull the fabric around to the back of the screen and fasten with staples, starting with opposite sides. Fold to create a mitered corner **(I)**.

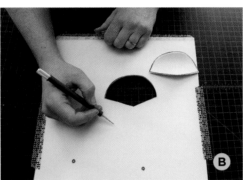

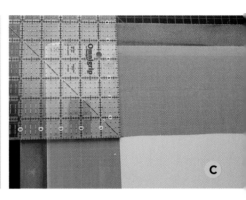

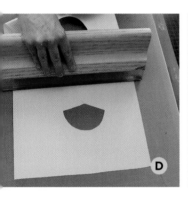

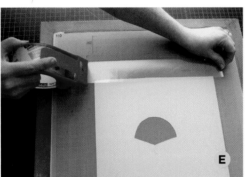

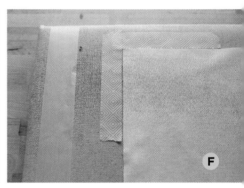

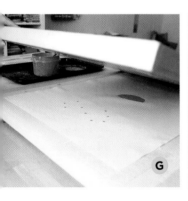

BEST FRIENDS
STUFFIES

Oh, the cuteness! This beaver and bunny duo are ready to take on the playroom. You can easily adapt the shape to create other animals — substitute the ears and tails to make maybe a kitty and bear pair. Or try making your own special design. It's all up to you and your imagination. Materials listed are for one stuffie.

Materials

Main fabric: 1 fat quarter (18" x 22")

Backing fabric: 1 fat quarter (18" x 22")

Polyfill stuffing

20" x 24" screen

Drawing fluid

Screen filler

Sharpie pen

Disappearing ink pen

Scissors

Coordinating cotton thread

Hand-sewing needle

Iron

CREATING

1. Enlarge and trace the bunny or beaver design (see pages 152, 153) onto a piece of wax paper using a Sharpie pen.

> **TIP:** When I started screen printing, my brother-in-law P.J. advised me to create designs in which the lines were no thinner than ones from a standard Sharpie marker. It's a good guideline to adhere to when using drawing fluid.

2. Paint the design onto the center of your screen with drawing fluid **(A)**. Allow to dry for approximately 40 minutes.

3. Coat your screen with screen filler **(B)**. Allow to dry for approximately 1–2 hours.

4. Rinse out the drawing fluid and let the screen dry and cure.

5. Print the design onto the middle of your main fabric fat quarter using the techniques on page 56 **(C, D)**.

SEWING

1. Place the animal print and backing fabric wrong sides together.

2. Draw a line about 1½" around the design using a disappearing ink marker. Cut the two stacked fabrics on this line with scissors **(E)**.

3. Flip the fabrics so they are right sides together. Stitch them together using a ½" seam allowance, leaving a 4" opening at the bottom.

4. Trim and notch any curves **(F)**. Press.

5. Turn the stuffie right sides out and carefully push out any seams using a blunt tool like a chopstick.

6. Stuff your animal with polyfill **(G)**.

7. Stitch the opening closed using a ladder stitch (see page 117) **(H)**.

> **TIP:** Part of the beauty of this stuffie is its simplicity. But don't be afraid to play around with extra embellishments! Consider painting within the design with fabric paints or adding some embroidery. The possibilities are endless!

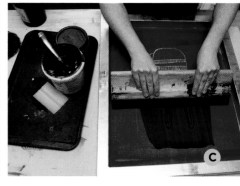

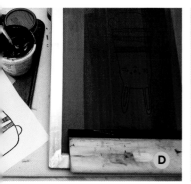

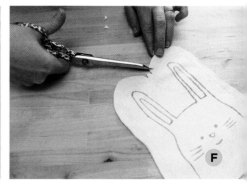

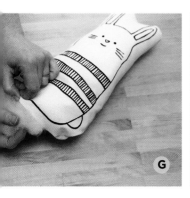

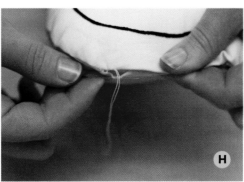

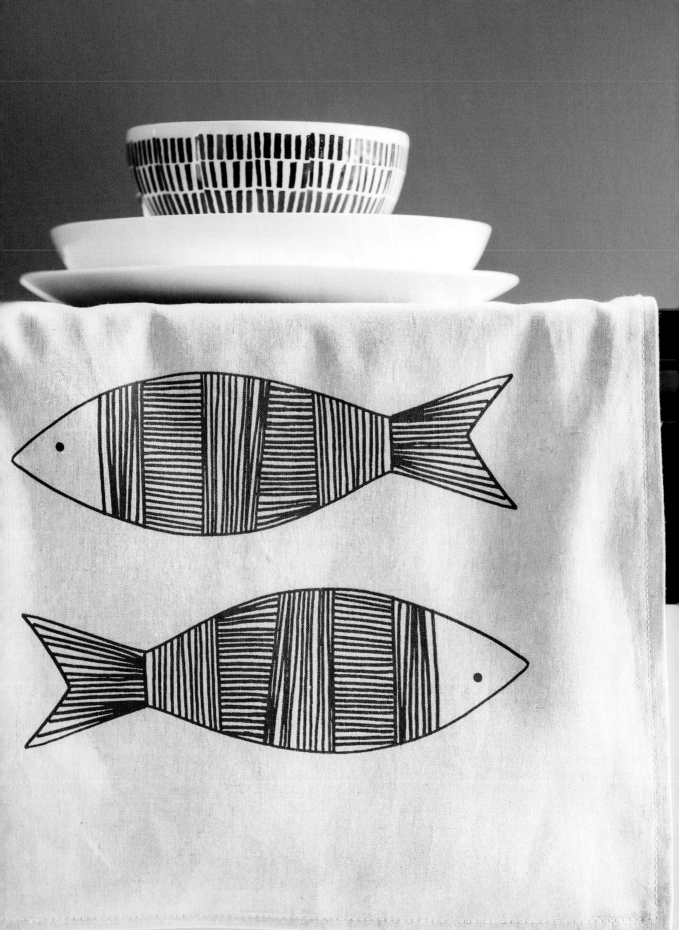

FISH MARKET
TABLE RUNNER

Once you have the hang of screen printing a single panel, why don't you give an easy repeat a try? This fish print is the perfect next step because there are no boxy edges — if the repeat isn't perfect, it will still look great. The secret is to take the time to mark your screen, your fabric, and your printing surface (see page 52). You can do it!

Finished Size: 15″ x 68″

Materials

2 yards linen/cotton blend or other midweight fabric

20″ x 24″ screen

Positive: fish images (see page 151) printed on an inkjet transparency

Screen printing ink

Squeegee

Scissors

Coordinating cotton thread

Masking tape

Disappearing ink pen

Iron

Cutting

From fabric, cut:
(1) 16″ x 69″ rectangle

(1) 18″ x 72″ rectangle

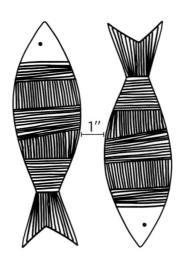

Figure 1

PREPARING THE FABRIC AND SCREEN

1. Wash, dry, and press your fabric.

2. Using the artwork on page 151, burn your screen (see page 56) **(A)**.

PRINTING REPEATS

> **TIP:** Printing repeats on fabric requires accurate alignment. When you are creating a design with the intention of repeating it, consider making one that doesn't have to line up perfectly to achieve the look the way you want.

1. Calculate the width of your repeat by measuring the width between the right and left edges of your design, and then adding the distance you want between the repeats; in this case, $7\frac{1}{2}'' + 1'' = 8\frac{1}{2}''$ **(B)**.

2. Mark this distance directly on the bottom of your screen frame with a disappearing ink pen **(C)**.

3. Lay a strip of masking tape along the bottom of your printing surface that will act as a line for placing your screen. Using the screen marks as your guide, mark the repeat distance directly on the strip of masking tape **(D)**.

4. Position your fabric on top of a flat surface and mark the repeats $8\frac{1}{2}''$ apart directly onto the fabric with a disappearing ink pen and begin printing (see page 52). When you print, you will line up your images to these marks. Depending on the length of your surface and the number of repeats, you will probably have to reposition the fabric to print the entire piece **(E)**.

5. In order to avoid smearing the ink with the screen when you do multiple prints: start by printing the first, third, fifth repeats, etc **(F)**; clean your screen and let everything dry; and then fill in your fabric with the second, fourth, sixth repeats, etc. **(G)**.

6. Let the ink dry for approximately 1 hour, then heat set with an iron (see page 20).

> **TIP:** When printing something where you might want a design to be centered, start marking the repeats at the center point of your fabric instead of at the left edge.

SEWING YOUR RUNNER

1. Center your design and trim the printed panel to 16″ x 69″

2. Lay the printed runner top and the backing fabric right sides facing together.

3. Stitch around the perimeter of the runner using a $\frac{1}{2}''$ seam allowance, leaving a 4″ opening on one side.

4. Press the seams to set the stitches and trim the corners to reduce the bulk **(H)**.

5. Turn the runner right side out and carefully push out the seams and corners using a blunt tool like a chopstick. Press flat.

6. Topstitch around the perimeter of the runner, being sure that you close the opening from Step 3 in the process **(I)**.

A

B

C

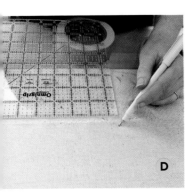

D

E

F

G

H

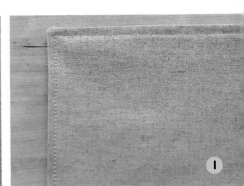

I

DYEING FABRIC

Dyeing your own fabric is another way to make your work unique. There is no limit to the colors you can create and it doesn't take a big investment in supplies. The dyeing techniques in this chapter allow for a lot of customization — you can play with color combinations and intensities in a fairly structured way. The dyeing process and supplies we will use are a long way from the grocery store dyes you may have used before.

THE BASICS

NATURAL FIBER FABRIC, PFD FABRIC

The dyes we use in these projects bond only to natural fabrics. This means cotton, wool, silk, hemp, etc. You can dye any fabric, but PFD (Prepared for Dyeing) fabrics "take" color best.

POWDERED MX PROCION DYES

Jacquard and Dharma Trading both carry lines of these dyes. They are easy to use and can be mixed with all water temperatures. Get a set of primary colors plus black to mix your own (see page 78). Before you do, though, check out the premixed selection: there are more than 130 colors to choose from!

SALT

Salt encourages the fabric to accept more of the dye. You can use basic table salt, but canning salt dissolves more quickly.

SODA ASH

This is used to fix the dye to your fabric. If you leave this out, the dyes do not hold. You can buy soda ash from an art supply store, online, or even at a pool supply shop.

SAFETY NOTE: Soda ash is a skin irritant, so wear gloves when handling it.

1-GALLON BUCKET

Buy an inexpensive one at the hardware store. A 1-gallon bucket is sturdy and has plenty of room for dyeing up to 2 yards of fabric. It's also easy to carry from your dyeing area to your laundry or wash-out room.

5-GALLON BUCKET

Buy this from the hardware store too. This larger size is good to use when rinsing out your fabric after you remove it from the dye bath.

RUBBER GLOVES

Pick up a pair of heavyweight dishwashing gloves at the grocery store, or longer ones from Dharma Trading if you think you'll go up to your elbows in your dye bucket.

STIRRING STICKS

These will be used to stir up your chemicals and dye, plus agitate the fabric during the dyeing process. Find something that's long enough to reach the bottom of your bucket. I use a long plastic spoon.

MEASURING CUPS AND SPOONS

Use these to measure chemicals and dyes. Get a set of spoons that goes down as small as $1/16$ of a teaspoon if you can.

> **SAFETY NOTE:** Once you use measuring cups and spoons for dye and chemicals, they should never be put back into your kitchen rotation for food. Keep separate sets that are *only* used for dyeing.

SYNTHRAPOL DETERGENT

This helps pull any remaining dye out of your fabric during the rinsing process.

RESPIRATOR FACE MASKS

You need to wear these when you are working with dyes in their powdered form. Otherwise you risk breathing in the chemicals — even the teensiest bit is not good for your lungs.

VINYL TABLECLOTH

Cut a square of this to cover your workstation when you are mixing dyes to protect your surface from stains.

OLD TOWELS

I like to use an old terrycloth towel, cut into washcloth-size pieces and dampened, to wipe down my vinyl tablecloth before I put it away. I also use the pieces to dry my rinsed cups, spoons, and bucket. It's a good idea to always have a stack handy when you start dyeing in case you need to quickly clean up a small spill.

THE DYE PROCESS

These instructions apply to dyeing **1 yard** of fabric. If you want to dye smaller or larger pieces, you will need to adjust the amounts of water, dye, soda ash and salt proportionately to get consistent results.

PREWASH YOUR FABRICS

It's important to wash your fabric before dyeing. Washing removes sizing and other chemicals that may interfere with the color taking hold. Even if you are using PFD fabrics, you still need to prewash your fabrics with synthrapol detergent to get out any dirt or oils that it can pick up after being handled. You can dry your fabric and save it for dyeing later — just don't use any fabric softeners or dryer sheets.

SET UP YOUR DYEING AREA

Place your supplies on your vinyl-covered work area. I place a folding table next to my utility sink or kitchen sink. Be sure that nothing comes into contact with food or anything that you use for cooking and eating.

PREPARE YOUR DYE BUCKET

Fill your 1-gallon bucket halfway up with warm to hot water. I set my bucket in the sink and leave it there during the entire dye process.

ADD YOUR CHEMICALS

I have come up with a simple formula for the amount of chemicals and dye I like to use for 1 yard of fabric:

½ GALLON WARM WATER + 1½ TBSP SODA ASH + 1 TBSP SALT + ½ TSP POWDERED DYE

Add 1½ tbsp of soda ash and 1 tbsp of salt to your water, stirring as you pour to keep the soda ash from clumping up on the bottom. Continue stirring until they are both dissolved **(A)**.

MIX YOUR DYE

SAFETY NOTE: Put on your respirator mask when handling powdered dye.

1. Scoop about a cup of your water solution from your bucket into a large cup or jar.

2. Put on your mask. Measure ½ tsp total of powdered dye and drop it into your cup of water solution. If you are mixing colors, make sure that the amounts added together equal ½ tsp (for instance, ¼ tsp yellow + ¼ tsp cobalt = ½ tsp total dye).

3. Carefully stir the dye powder into the solution until it appears the powder has completely dissolved. **(B)**. Once the dye powder is mixed into the solution, it is safe to remove your mask.

4. Pour the mixed dye solution into the bucket with the water solution and stir to completely mix it in.

5. Shake out your fabric and place it in the dye bath, loosely layering it in until it is completely submerged. Push it down and move it around with your hands or stir stick to make sure there are no air pockets trapped inside the folds of fabric **(C)**.

6. Stir your fabric every 10 minutes or so. While you wait, half fill a 5-gallon bucket with cold water.

7. After 30–45 minutes, remove the fabric from the dye bath and place it in the cold water bucket. Swish the fabric through the water and squeeze it repeatedly to remove the extra dye.

8. Wash out your 1-gallon bucket. Place your fabric back inside and use it to carry your wet fabric to your washing machine.

9. Wash the fabric on a hot cycle with 1 tsp of synthrapol. Dry in your dryer. Take it out while it's still damp and iron.

GETTING THE COLOR YOU WANT

There are many variables to consider when determining how to obtain a certain color. It helps to be relaxed about the outcome and have fun experimenting with combinations. Some factors to consider are:

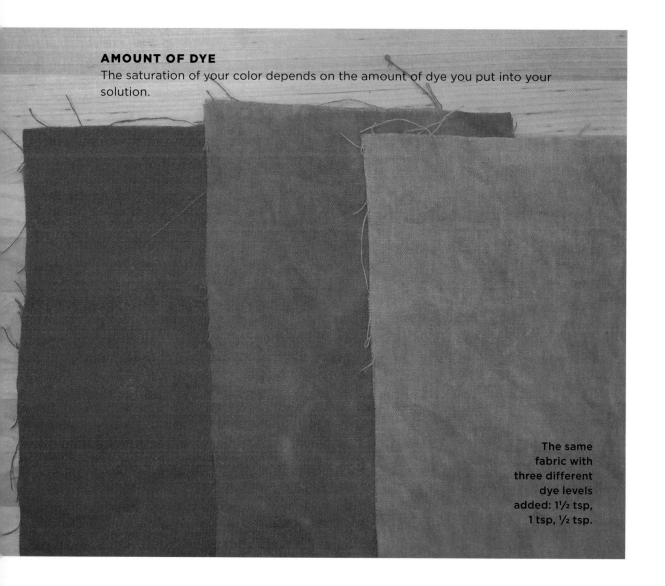

AMOUNT OF DYE
The saturation of your color depends on the amount of dye you put into your solution.

The same fabric with three different dye levels added: 1½ tsp, 1 tsp, ½ tsp.

TIME

The color will intensify the longer the fabric sits in the dye bath.

The same fabric and same dye level, left in the dye bath for 3 hours, 60 minutes, and 30 minutes.

BASE FABRIC

The same dye bath can have different results on different fabrics. Notice how the aqua dye appears more green on the natural canvas.

Four different fabrics with the same dye level and dye bath time: Essex Natural, Canvas, Essex PFD White, PFD Jersey Knit.

DOUBLE TAKE
DYED NAPKINS

In my house, we can never have enough napkins. Because of this, cloth napkins are the perfect projects for my dye experiments. A set of four napkins uses 2 yards of fabric. I like to use one color on one side, and one color on the other. This is a great way to experiment with color mixes, dyeing times or chemical concentrations of your own.

Finished Size:
16" square

Materials

PFD cotton muslin fabric: 2 yards

Procion MX dyes

Coordinating or contrasting cotton thread

Iron

DYEING THE FABRIC

1. Prewash your fabric in synthrapol.

2. Cut the 2 yards of fabric into (4) ½ yard pieces. Dye your four fabrics in four separate dye baths.

3. Wash, dry, and press.

4. Repeat Steps 1–3 with a variety of dye formulas to create a total of (8) 17″ dyed squares.

SEWING

1. Place one square of each color fabric right sides together **(A)**.

2. Stitch around the perimeter of the square using a ½″ seam allowance, leaving a 3″ opening on one side **(B)**.

3. Press the seams to set the stitches and trim the corners.

4. Turn the napkin right side out and press out the seams and corners with a blunt object like a chopstick.

5. Topstitch around the perimeter of the napkin, closing up the opening in the process **(C)**.

6. Repeat Steps 1–5 to create a total of 4 napkins.

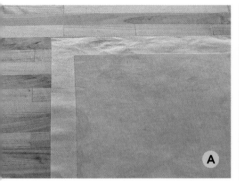

CARMINE RED

RASPBERRY

½ tsp bright
scarlet + ½ tsp
lemon yellow

COBALT BLUE

½ tsp cobalt
blue + ½ tsp
lemon yellow

½ tsp antique
gold + 1/16 tsp
chocolate brown

ROBIN'S
EGG BLUE

½ tsp lemon
yellow + a few
grains of jet
black

EMERALD GREEN

AVOCADO

RIVET TUFTED
PILLOW

This fresh take on a custom-dyed tufted pillow uses metal rivets and a quick and easy way to get them in there. (Hint: You won't be trying to hammer rivets through a bunch of stuffing.) The rivets are a subtle design element that pairs nicely with using hand-dyed fabrics for both the front and back of the pillow.

Materials

¾ yard of PFD fabric

1 yard medium-weight fusible woven interfacing

4 medium ($\frac{5}{16}$") metal rivets

Polyester stuffing

Procion MX dyes

Disappearing ink pen

2mm leather hole punch

Fray check

Coordinating thread

Scissors

Iron

Cutting

From dyed fabric, cut:
(2) 13" x 25" rectangles

From interfacing, cut:
(2) 13" x 25" rectangles

DYEING THE FABRIC

1. Prewash your fabric in synthrapol.

2. Dye the fabric your desired color (see page 75). In this example, I used a dye formula of $\frac{1}{2}$ tsp cobalt blue + $\frac{1}{2}$ tsp lemon yellow for the 1 yard of fabric.

3. Wash, dry, and press.

SEWING

1. Iron the interfacing to the wrong sides of both rectangles of fabric **(A)**.

2. Place the two fabric rectangles right sides together. Pin.

3. Sew together using a $\frac{1}{2}$" seam allowance, making sure to leave a 6" opening in the center of the bottom long side **(B)**.

4. Trim the corners, turn the pillow right side out press out the corners with a blunt object like a chopstick, and press flat.

5. With a disappearing ink pen, on the front side of the pillow place marks centered 6" from the top and the bottom at these locations from the left side: 4", 9", 15", and 20" **(C)**.

6. Punch a hole through both layers of the pillow at each mark using a 2mm leather punch **(D)**.

7. Put a small amount of fray check around the edges of each hole, on both sides of the pillow **(E)**.

8. Install rivets (see page 96) in the punched holes **(F)**.

9. Stuff your pillow with polyester stuffing, starting at the top corners and working down the sides and to the center. Work gently around the rivets to keep from ripping the fabric **(G)**.

10. Once your pillow is fully stuffed, hand stitch the bottom opening closed using a ladder stitch (see page 117) **(H)**.

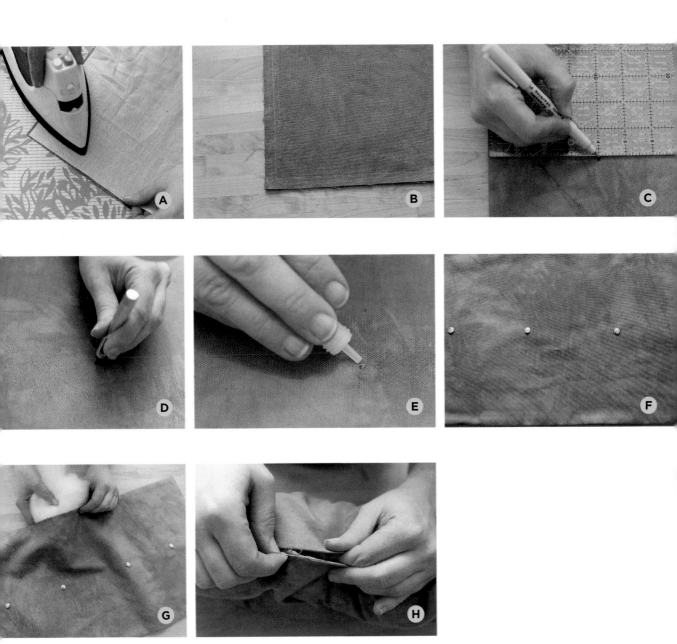

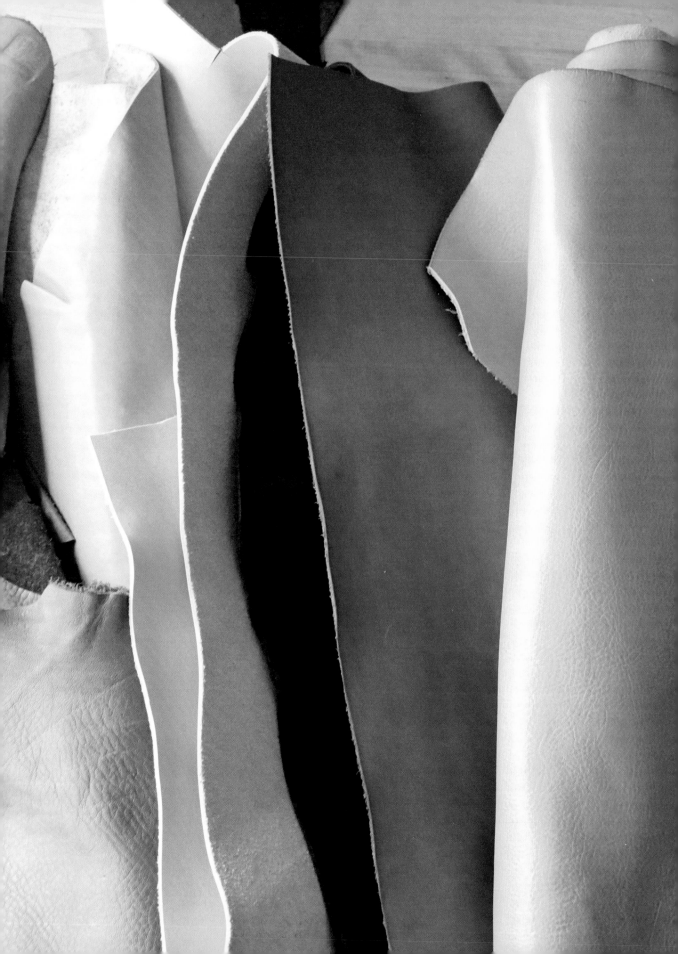

LEATHER

It's time to do some experimenting with materials outside of fabric! These lessons will teach you techniques for working successfully with leather and luxuriously thick wool felt, plus you'll learn how to apply bias tape in two different ways. You'll also learn how to install metal rivets and eyelets.

BUYING LEATHER

It can be really intimidating to purchase leather at first. It's expensive, it's measured in a completely different way than fabric and there are so many options.

When you enter a leather shop, you will see shelves lined with rolled up or flat stacks of all different kinds of leather. The leather will likely be labeled with its weight in ounces and its type. Unlike fabric stores where you have your fabric cut to your determined yardage, leather shops don't cut you pieces from a hide. You buy the whole piece from the shelf.

Each piece of leather will be different. It will have different markings, coloring, and shape. Pull the hide out, open it up, and check to see if there are any imperfections that will affect your project. Look at its weight, but also feel how it drapes. Does it fold easily? How much does it stretch?

LEATHER WEIGHT

Because most of us will be using a domestic sewing machine, don't purchase any leather more than 3 oz. in weight. Save the heavier weights for bag straps, baskets and bracelets.

> **TIP:** I prefer to use real leather, but if that's not an option for you, the methods that are used to sew with leather can be applied to "vegan" leather too.

MARKING AND CUTTING LEATHER

Before you begin cutting your leather, it's important to look over the hide again to see if there are any previously unseen defects (such as holes or uneven texture) that you might not want on your finished piece. If you find something that you don't like, mark it from the back so you can avoid it when cutting later.

Mark where you want to cut directly on the leather using a chalk pen if you'll be seeing the raw edges, but you can use a fine permanent marker if the cut edges won't be exposed.

Cut straight edges of leather using a rotary cutter and ruler. I use my acrylic quilting rulers, but you can also use a cork-backed metal ruler. Make sure that your rotary cutter blade is held straight up and down, not at an angle as you cut, especially on thicker leathers.

LEATHER SUPPLIES

1 NYLON OR POLYESTER THREAD

When you sew with leather, don't use cotton thread — it just isn't strong enough and will break down over time. Use nylon or polyester. The weight often depends on what you're stitching. When I topstitch, I like to use a heavier weight upholstery thread (Gutterman or Coats & Clark both have good ones), but I leave a standard weight polyester thread in the bobbin to help keep my tension from getting funky. When stitching together thinner leather pieces, I use general weight polyester in both the bobbin and the top thread (I like Coats & Clark Double Duty XP).

2 SEWING MACHINE NEEDLES

Use sewing machine needles specifically made for stitching with leather. I usually have Schmetz 110/18 leather needles handy for topstitching, and 90/14 needles for when I'm attaching leather pieces together (it makes smaller holes).

HAND STITCHING NEEDLES

Use a leather needle when you need to pull threads to the back of your leather.

3 CLOVER WONDER CLIPS

These are a must in any sewing basket. You cannot use pins when sewing with leather because it will create permanent holes in your project. Buy a pack of these clips for securing layers together.

4 WASH AWAY WONDER TAPE

This is also a must in your sewing basket that I use for more than just sewing with leather. When I am using leather, I use Wonder Tape for temporarily securing the leather to zippers and fabric before I sew.

5 DOUBLE-SIDED TAPE

This is a sturdier, more permanent tape used to hold layers together in seams.

6 CHALK PEN OR FINE TIP PERMANENT MARKER

Use this to mark on the back of your leather before you cut it.

7 LEATHER GLUE

Use this to keep seams flattened and to attach pieces of leather to each other. Rubber cement is commonly used, but I like a liquid product called Tear Mender.

8 LEATHER PAINTS

These are special paints that bond to leather. You can mix them like other paints to get custom colors. My favorite brand is Eco Flow because it goes on smoothly with an opaque finish and it dries very quickly.

> **CAN YOUR SEWING MACHINE HANDLE LEATHER?** I sew with a Juki TI-2000, which is a non-computerized, semi-industrial machine. It handles leather beautifully. But even a domestic sewing machine can stitch through leather. Just make sure you are using the correct needle, and go slowly when sewing! Using the hand wheel to manually make stitches over thick areas can make the task much easier for you and your machine.

WALKING FOOT

I always use the walking foot on my machine when I sew with leather. It feeds all the layers very evenly and helps keep stretching to a minimum.

9 HEAVY SHEARS

Get a pair of heavy shears for cutting your leather. You'll want to use these rather than a rotary cutter for smaller, more precise cuts. Padded handles provide comfort when you have to cut through very thick leather.

10 ROTARY CUTTER

Use a 45mm rotary cutter to cut straight edges. I love my rotary cutter from Lee Valley Tools. It has a metal handle and its shape is easier on my wrists.

11 SKIVING TOOL

This is essentially a razor blade set in a curved handle that allows you to shave off layers of leather to reduce bulk (see page 95).

12 EDGE BEVELING TOOL

Use this for rounding the edges of thicker leather in bracelets, belts, and straps.

13 POLY OR RAWHIDE MALLET

Since you can't iron leather, use this specialty hammer to flatten out seams. You'll also use this to punch holes, set rivets and eyelets, and emboss with metal stamps.

GLOVER'S NEEDLE

Use this to pull threads to the back or inside of your work when you tie off threads.

14 HOLE PUNCHES

You can get a rotating plier-style punch or individual punches that you use with a hammer. You can't beat the convenience of the plier model, but the individual punches are more versatile. I like having both.

THICK PLASTIC CUTTING BOARD

Use this underneath your leather when you are punching holes to protect your work surface.

15 RIVET SETTER

Purchase a rivet tool to set your rivets. This tool consists of a two-sided circular anvil, one side flat and one side concave, and a metal rod with a flat and concave end.

16 EYELET SETTER

Like a rivet setter, this consists of a circular anvil and a metal rod that has a flat end and a tapered end. You use this with a mallet to set eyelets in your fabric.

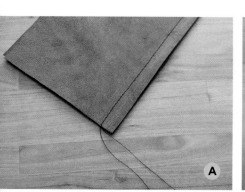

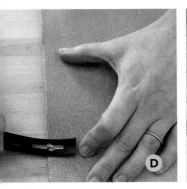

IMPORTANT TECHNIQUES

TIE OFF YOUR THREADS

When sewing fabric, the tried and true way to secure stitches is to backstitch at the beginning and end of a seam. Unfortunately, this is not a good practice with leather. Get used to leaving long thread tails at the beginning and end of your seams **(A)**, pull them to the inside of your project if applicable, and knot them securely **(B)**. Trim the threads and secure the knot by quickly melting it with a match or lighter flame **(C)**.

SKIVING

Skiving your seam allowances is a good way to reduce bulk when you are sewing multiple layers of leather together. To skive, position your piece of leather so that the seam goes vertically away from your body. If you are right-handed, hold the top edge of the leather with your left hand, and hold the skiver with your right so the blade is perpendicular **(D)**.

Place the blade along the edge of your leather, angle it down slightly, and begin pulling down in short strokes **(E)**. You can go over areas more than once, but don't shave off more than half of the leather's thickness.

BEVELING

A beveling tool rounds off the edges of your thicker leather strips by removing the 90 degree edge. To use a beveling tool, lay your leather strip on a flat surface. Hold it stable with your free hand. Hold the beveling tool at a 30-degree angle at the bottom of your strip so that it hugs the corner. Apply light pressure and push the tool away from you. A very small strip of leather will be shaved off as you go **(F)**.

RIVETS

Rivets add strength to joins in leather projects, especially when it comes to attaching bag handles. They also solve a problem when layers are too thick to stitch using a machine, or add a purely decorative accent.

Double cap rivets have a round dome on both sides. Rapid rivets have a flat head on one side and a donut shape on the other side.

Rapid rivets   Double cap rivets

Determine the appropriate size rivet by measuring the thickness of where you plan to set it. You want the rivet to be snug — a too-long rivet tends to "walk" to one side when you set it.

SETTING A RIVET

1. Punch a hole in your material where you plan to place your rivet. When I rivet handles onto my bags, I punch holes in the handle first and then use the handles as a template to punch holes in the bag itself **(A)**.

2. Insert the part of the rivet with the stem through the front side of your project and through the layers to the back. Place the cap on the rivet stem on the back side of your project and give it a squeeze to temporarily lock the rivet together **(B)**.

3. Place the round anvil on a hard surface such as a scrap piece of granite or a concrete floor. (If you are using rapid rivets, put the flat side of the anvil facing up. If you are using double cap rivets, put the concave side facing up.) Place the cap end of the rivet on top of the anvil. Hold the metal rod so the concave end rests on top of the rivet **(C)**.

4. Tap the top of the metal rod with your mallet a few times to set the rivet. You don't have to put a lot of pressure on it.

A

B

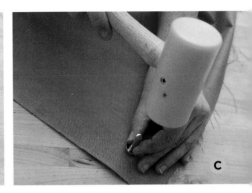

EYELETS

Eyelets are metal circles that are used to protect a hole cut in material such as fabric or leather. They help laces or straps slide through more easily and keep the edges of the hole from fraying or stretching.

SETTING AN EYELET

1. Determine the size of the eyelet you need by considering the thickness of what will need to pass through it. You want the lace or strap to pass through smoothly. If you are securing a strap with a knotted end, such as in the Bias Tape Bound Apron (p. 142), you will also want to make sure that the eyelet is not so large that the knot can pass through.

2. Determine where you want to place your eyelet.

3. Trace the inside of the eyelet onto the material and cut the area out carefully with scissors **(A)**.

4. Place the post end of the eyelet through the hole from the front of your project. Place the washer over the end from the back **(B)**.

5. Place the eyelet on the anvil with the post facing up and the other end up toward you. Place the tapered end of the eyelet tool into the open end of the post **(C)**.

6. Tap the top of the eyelet tool with your mallet a few times to set the eyelet.

LEATHER
HEXAGON PILLOW

Using leather shapes in an appliqué method is a great way to get acquainted with sewing leather. Because leather doesn't fray, all you have to worry about are your stitches. Pair it with a matching rubber stamp and you can create a really fun pattern that alternates both forms!

Materials

Pillow front fabric: 1 fat quarter (18″ x 22″) of a linen, canvas, or off-white solid

Backing fabric: 1 fat quarter (18″ x 22″)

Woven medium-weight fusible interfacing: ½ yard based on 20″ wide

Leather: 2–3 oz., at least 12″ square

16″ pillow form

Screen printing ink

Ink pad

Rubber carving material

Disappearing ink pen

Hexagon template (see page 154)

Wonder tape

Coordinating upholstery-weight polyester thread

Coordinating cotton thread

Iron

Cutting

From your pillow front fabric, cut:
(1) 16½″ square

From your backing fabric, cut:
(2) 16½″ x 11″ rectangles

From your interfacing, cut:
(1) 16½″ square

From your leather, cut:
(8) hexagons from template (see page 154)

CARVING THE BLOCK

1. Trace the hexagon template onto tracing paper using a pencil.

2. Transfer your design to the rubber carving material. (see page 33).

3. Carve your block and mount it to plexiglass if preferred (see page 36) **(A)**.

PRINTING AND STITCHING THE HEXAGONS

1. Iron the interfacing to the wrong side of your pillow front fabric square.

2. Mark your hexagon design on the pillow front using a disappearing ink pen and the original template from Step 1 of *Carving the Block* and set aside **(B)**.

3. Repeat Step 2 using the leather **(C)**.

4. Place a few strips of wonder tape along the back of each leather hexagon **(D)**.

5. Referencing Figure 1 (right), place and secure the leather hexagons one at a time by edgestitching the leather to the pillow front. Using your upholstery-weight thread, begin sewing at one corner of the hexagon and work slowly, making sure the sewing machine needle is in the down position when you pivot at each corner. Repeat with the remaining leather hexagons.

6. Make an ink pad (see page 34) and test your block on a piece of scrap fabric.

7. Print your hexagons being sure to rotate the stamp to vary the orientation of the design to create interest **(E)**.

> **TIP:** Begin with long thread tails before stitching each of the leather hexagons. At the end, cut long tails and pull the threads to the back to knot and trim.

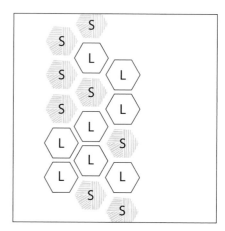

Figure 1

8. Once the disappearing ink from Step 2 has completely gone, carefully heat set (see page 20) the stamped-on ink.

ASSEMBLING THE PILLOW

1. On each backing rectangle, press ¼" of one long side wrong sides together, then press ¼" again to make a hem **(F)**. Topstitch using cotton thread.

2. Position the pillow front facing up. Position the backing pieces right sides down so they overlap across the center of the pillow **(G)**. Pin the layers together.

3. Sew around the entire perimeter of the pillow using a ½" seam allowance **(H)**.

> **TIP:** Serge or zig zag stitch over the raw edges before trimming and turning the pillow right side out. This prevents fraying.

4. Trim your corners. Turn the pillow right side out, then carefully push out the corners using a blunt object lik a chopstick and press.

5. Insert your pillow form through the opening in the back **(I)**.

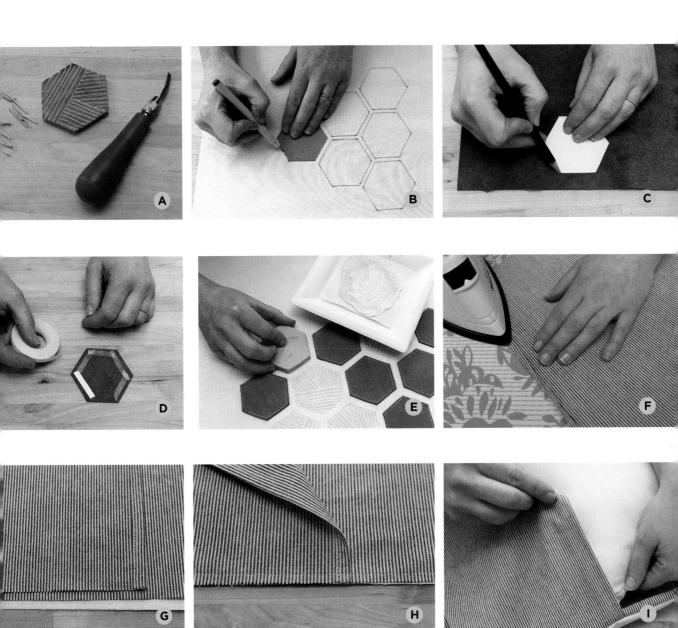

LEATHER BRACELETS,
THREE DIFFERENT WAYS

Leather bracelets are quick to make and fun for gifting. I'll show you how to embellish them in three different ways — carved, stitched and block printed — to make each bracelet unique. Varying the width of the leather creates even more possibilities. This is a great project to do with a group of friends. The materials listed below will be used in each embellishment project.

Materials

Leather: 5–8 oz., strips or belt blanks

Rotary cutter

Edge beveler

3.5 mm leather hole punch

Leather snaps and snap setter (see tip)

TIP: Leather snaps are different from the type you would use on fabric. Leather snaps are inserted through a hole that is punched in the leather, while fabric snaps are attached using prongs that go through the fabric.

CUTTING

1. Measure the wrist of the person who will wear the bracelet. Add 1″ to this measurement. Using a rotary cutter, cut your leather strip to this length.

2. For width, I recommend anywhere between ½″ and 1½″. This is a good general rule for comfort and allows enough room to insert a closure. Using a rotary cutter, cut your leather strip to the desired width.

3. At this point you can also trim the corners of your bracelet ends with a rotary cutter. Do a deeper corner for a wider bracelet and just a slight nip for a narrow one **(A)**.

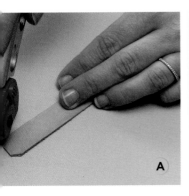

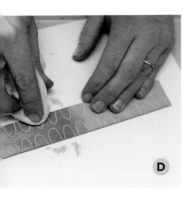

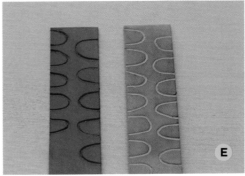

EMBELLISHING

CARVING

Additional Supplies

Lino cutter set

Pencil or needle

Acrylic or leather paint (optional)

1. Position your strap on a firm flat surface. Lightly draw a design by scratching the leather with the end of a needle, or transfer a design with pencil as you would for a rubber block **(B)**.

2. Use the small V gouge in your lino cutter set to carve details into the top of the bracelet, making sure not to cut too deeply **(C)**. The leather cuts differently than a rubber block, but as long as you just barely skim the surface, it shouldn't be too difficult.

3. If you want to add some color, rub a bit of acrylic or leather paint into the carved areas and on the edges of the leather with a paper towel. Quickly wipe off the excess paint with a clean paper towel to leave just the carved design covered with paint **(D)**.

4. As an alternative, rub a bit of leather conditioner on the bracelet to highlight the carving in a subtle way. You can also color your leather with leather paint before carving **(E)**.

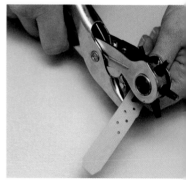

BLOCK PRINTING

Additional Supplies

Rubber carving material

Lino cutters

Dye-based ink pad

Leather paint (optional)

1. Carve your rubber material with your own design or use an existing design, such as the artwork on page 154.

2. Print your design across the leather. Let it dry for approximately 10 minutes **(F)**.

3. Embellish with leather paint if desired.

> **TIP:** Block printing on leather is a bit like block printing on coated paper — the ink sits on the surface instead of sinking in. Because of that, I've found that dye-based ink pads (as opposed to the pigment-based ink pads or screen printing inks I suggest for printing on fabric) are a better option for leather and still stay permanent.

STITCHING

Additional Supplies

Embroidery floss or size 8 perle cotton

Embroidery needle

Awl

2 mm hole punch

1. Trace your leather strap onto a piece of paper and sketch a design for your stitching to use as a template, or use the template on page 154.

2. Place the paper template on top of your leather strap and poke through the paper with an awl to mark where you will punch your holes **(G)**.

3. Punch holes in each mark using a 2 mm hole punch **(H)**.

4. Thread your embroidery needle with floss and tie a knot. Bring your first stitch up through the back of one hole and down through the next. On the back side of the bracelet, take a stitch through the knot to secure it before going back to the front side **(I)**.

5. Continue stitching until your design is complete. Knot the end on the under side of the bracelet. Trim excess floss.

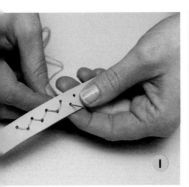  

ATTACHING A SNAP CLOSURE

1. Punch a 3.5 mm hole centered and ½" from each end of your bracelet **(J)**.

2. Attach a leather-appropriate snap using instructions that come with the snap setter **(K)**.

FINISHING AND FORMING

For a more finished look, you can use the edge beveler to soften the edges of your bracelet (see page 104).

To get the bracelet to conform to the round shape of your wrist, soak it for 5 minutes in a bowl of warm water. Close the snap, shape the bracelet with your hands and let it dry overnight.

WHAT TYPE OF LEATHER SHOULD YOU BUY?

Veg Tan Leather: Veg Tan is natural in color and can be stained, stamped, and painted easily because of its smooth texture. With time and use, it develops a darker patina that can be very beautiful. Since it's a bit more stiff, I like to use veg tan leather for bracelets, accents, and straps. Milled veg tan leather has the same natural color but is more supple and textured.

Deertan Leather: Deertan is actually cowhide that is tanned to look like deerskin. It's soft and supple, and a bit stretchy. I like to use this in conjunction with other materials in pouches, bags, and applique.

Top Grain Leather: Top grain is a higher quality leather that usually has a uniform color and waxy finish. I like to use this in tote bags and items that need a bit more structure.

Leather Weight: Stick to leathers that are 2-4 ounces in weight when you are stitching them on a domestic sewing machine. 5-8 ounce leathers are best for bracelets and straps.

PAINTED LEATHER
BASKET

This no-sew project is quick and easy. All it takes is a cut of a template, some punching, and two rivets. If you don't want to paint it, you can leave the leather raw or even stamp it! You can also substitute in 3 mm felt for the leather. The templates come in three sizes, so make a set to hold all your goodies in style!

Materials

4–5 oz. veg tan leather (see page 107):
6″ x 7½″ (small basket), 8″ x 10″ (medium basket), or 10″ x 12½″ (large basket)

Leather paint

1″ nylon paintbrush

3mm leather punch

Rubber mallet

Low-tack masking tape

Chalk pen

Heavy shears

(2) ½″ rivets

Rivet setter

PAINTING

1. Attach a piece of low-tack masking or painter's tape to the top of the leather at an angle with the oustide edge of the tape approximately 3″ away from the top left corner. Press the tape flat with your finger to seal down the edges **(A)**.

2. Use a soft 1″ nylon brush to paint your leather paint in an even coat across one half of the leather. Repeat if you need more coverage **(B)**.

3. Remove the masking tape and allow the paint to dry.

CUTTING

1. Cut out the template (see page 155).

2. Trace the outline of the template onto the back of your leather with chalk and transfer the hole markings.

3. Punch holes with a 3.5 mm punch through the 6 markings from Step 2 **(C)**.

> **TIP:** It can be tough cutting all the way into the inside corner in thicker leather using only shears. It helps to punch a small hole in the corner first and cut the lines to it.

4. Using your heavy shears, carefully cut out your leather **(D)**.

ASSEMBLING

1. On one end, fold each pointed corner over to the outside of the square flap, overlapping each piece so that the holes align **(E)**.

2. Insert a rivet and set it with the rivet setting tool (see page 96) **(F)**.

3. Repeat Steps 1–2 with the other side of the basket.

LEATHER BOTTOM
ZIPPER POUCH

This is the first project I ever made using leather. I loved the idea of mixing my screen prints with something a bit hardier. When you sew this pouch, you'll learn helpful tricks for combining fabric with leather, sewing two pieces of leather together and sewing a metal zipper to ensure clean corners at the top of the pouch.

Materials

Exterior fabric: 1 panel of screen printed or painted fabric, measuring at least 9" x 11"

Lining fabric: 1 fat quarter (18" x 22")

Leather: 2–3 oz., measuring at least 7" x 11"

Leather shears

Skiver

Coordinating cotton thread

Coordinating upholstery-weight polyester thread

Leather sewing machine needle

Zipper foot

Wonder clips

Iron

Fusible fleece interfacing: ¼ yard

9" metal zipper

Cutting

From leather, cut:
(2) 3" x 10½" rectangles

(1) ⅛" x 8" rectangle for the zipper pull

From exterior fabric, cut:
(2) 4" x 10½" rectangles

From fusible fleece, cut:
(2) 3¼" x 10" rectangles

From lining, cut:
(2) 6¼" x 10½" rectangles

PREPARING

LEATHER

1. To round the bottom corners of the leather rectangles, take a round object the size of a coffee mug or drinking glass and trace around it on the bottom corners of each leather piece. Trim along this line with leather shears to create rounded bottom corners **(A)**.

2. Skive the edges (see page 95) of each leather piece to reduce bulk in the seam allowances **(B)**.

LINING

Repeat Step 1 from the leather instructions above to round the bottom corners of your two lining pieces.

EXTERIOR FABRIC

1. Iron a rectangle of fusible fleece to the wrong side of each of the exterior fabric rectangles according to the product directions, centering each piece of fleece $1/2''$ from the top raw edge of each rectangle. There will be $1/4''$ of space on the sides and bottom **(C)**.

2. Fold the top raw edge of the exterior rectangles $1/2''$ to the wrong side (fold should be at the edge of the fusible fleece) and press **(D)**.

ZIPPER

It's much easier to attach a zipper when both ends are secured. Before you begin sewing, stitch together the open end of the zipper using your machine or a few hand stitches **(E)**.

SEWING MACHINE

Be sure to install a leather needle and an upholstery-weight thread in your machine if sewing through thick leather.

SEWING

MAKING THE EXTERIOR PANELS

1. Place the long side of your leather and unfolded edge of the exterior panel right sides together. Sew using a stitch length of 3. It can be helpful to attach the exterior panel with the leather on top, so the leather doesn't stick to the bed of your machine **(F)**.

2. Flatten out the pieced panel and finger press the seam so that the leather piece is lying flat **(G)**.

3. Topstitch the fabric along the seam **(H)**.

ASSEMBLING THE POUCH

1. On your work surface, position one lining piece right side up.

2. Align the zipper, facing up, on the long edge of the lining fabric. Pin as shown. Unzip the zipper about halfway **(I)**.

3. Align the folded edge of your exterior panel right side up on top of the zipper, so that the fold is about $1/8''$ from the zipper teeth. Using your zipper foot, topstitch the exterior panel along the zipper through all the layers. When you get to the zipper pull, leave your sewing machine needle in the down position and move the zipper pull up out of your way **(J)**.

4. Repeat Step 3 for the other side of the pouch **(K)**.

5. Open your zipper about $2/3$ of the way.

6. Fold both the linings and exterior panels away from the zipper so that they face each other right sides together (lining to lining, exterior to exterior) **(L)**. Secure the two pieces with Wonder Clips. You can also pin the layers of the lining together, but this will leave permanent holes in the leather.

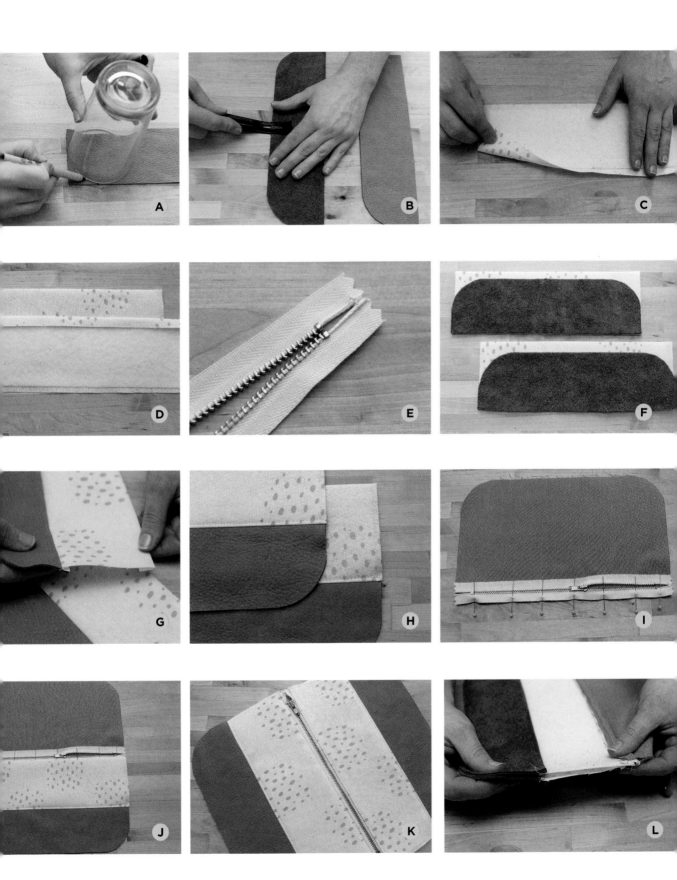

7. Starting at a point on the bottom long edge, sew the exterior panels together along the bottom and up one side using a $\frac{3}{8}$" seam allowance. Stop sewing when you get to the stitch line that marks where the lining panel is attached to the zipper. Backstitch to secure your stitches **(M)**. Repeat on the other side of the pouch.

> **A NOTE ON STITCH LENGTH:** When you are sewing the leather portion, make sure to sew it with a 3–3.5 stitch length. When you get to the fabric portion, change your stitch length to 2.

8. Leaving a 4" opening along the bottom of the lining, sew the lining panels together along the bottom and up one side using a $\frac{1}{4}$" seam allowance. Stop sewing when you get about $\frac{1}{4}$" from the stitch line that marks where the lining is sewn to the zipper. (You will also feel the bulk of the zipper in front of your presser foot as you get close to that point.) Backstitch to secure. Repeat on the other side of the pouch.

9. Turn your pouch right side out through the opening from Step 8. Gently press the seams out of both the exterior and lining panels using a blunt object like a chopstick, including the corners by the zipper ends, so that they all lie flat. Hammer the leather seams to flatten, and press the fabric.

10. Using a ladder stitch (see page 117) sew the opening in the lining closed. Tuck it into your pouch **(N)**.

11. Slip your leather strip through the hole in the zipper pull and knot to finish **(O)**.

> **SEWING A POUCH USING ANY SIZE ZIPPER:** What do you do if you don't have a 9" zipper? It's easy to adjust the size of your pouch to fit your zipper using this simple formula: Zipper Size + $1\frac{1}{2}$" = Width of Cut Fabric

THE LADDER STITCH

1. Thread needle, tying thread tails together in a knot at end to form a doubled thread for stitching. sew a stitch into project back at the outer edge, within the seam allowance. This hides your knot **(A)**.

2. Insert needle into one side of the fabric hem and exit just outside the opposite side.

3. insert needle into the hem fold of the opposite hem directly above your stitch. Push needle along ¼" inside the hem and exit within the hem **(B)**.

4. Insert needle just outside the hem on ths same side as step 1 Push needle along ¼". Take care to avoid the needle going through to project front. the needle is primarily positioned parallel to fabric rather than being inserted straight into and out of fabric **(C)**.

5. Pull gently on your thread to cinch the opening closed. Knot when finished and burry the knot through the hem before cutting the thread **(D)**.

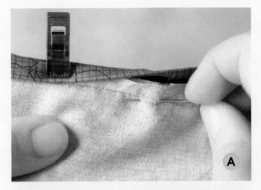

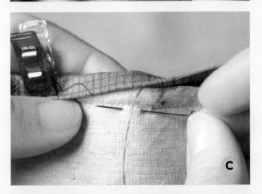

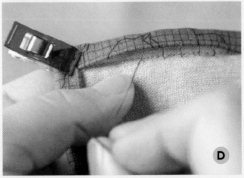

LEATHER
WRAPPED
WOOL CLUTCH

Thick wool felt (also known as industrial grade felt) is such a dream to sew with — like leather, it doesn't fray, and it feels luxurious in the hand. It also provides padding to a phone or tablet case. Combining felt with leather makes for a rich look that can appeal to both men and women. Materials listed are for one clutch

Materials

3 mm thick wool felt: 9" x 18"

1" square scrap of regular felt

Leather: 2-3 oz., at least 1¼" x 18½"

Coordinating general weight polyester thread for the leather

Coordinating general weight polyester thread for the wool

Wonder tape

Leather hole punches (2.3 mm, 3.5 mm, and 4 mm sizes)

Large button stud closure

Chalk pen

Leather needle

Wonder clips

Matches or a lighter

Acrylic ruler

CUTTING

1. On one of the short ends, trace the curved template (see page 156) and trim **(A)**.

2. Cut your leather to measure 1¼" x 18½".

ATTACHING THE STRAP

1. Mark a vertical line on the right side of the felt, 4½" from one side, with a chalk pen **(B)**.

2. Align wonder tape along each wrong side of the leather strip on the long edges, leaving the last 2½" of the end of your strap without tape **(C)**.

3. Align the leather strip along the center of the felt, beginning at the straight short end and using the chalk line as a guide to keep it centered. (2" of leather should overhang the curved edge of the felt.)

4. Test your thread tension on your sewing machine using a scrap of leather and felt and adjust the tension if necessary.

5. Install the leather needle and upholstery-weight polyester thread in your sewing maching. Beginning at the straight short side, slowly edgestitch the leather to the felt, ⅛" away from the edge of the leather. When you get to the curved edge, pivot and stitch straight across your strap. Pivot again and continue down the other side of the strap **(D)**.

6. Pull threads to the wrong side of the felt, knot, and melt to secure (see page 95).

7. Mark a spot 4½" from the straight short edge of the clutch piece, centered in the leather strap. Make a hole using a 3.5 mm leather punch **(E)**.

8. Insert the button stud and tighten with a screwdriver **(F)**.

> **TIP:** If you are going to use this for a tablet or other device, fasten the piece of scrap felt over the top of the screw back with a bit of fabric glue to prevent it from scratching the screen.

SEWING THE CLUTCH

1. Fold the straight short edge of the felt wrong sides together up to where the overlap measures 6". Secure the two layers together with Wonder Clips **(G)**.

2. Sew each side from the fold to the top edge using a ⅛" seam allowance, backstitching at the beginning and end to secure the stitches **(H)**.

3. Fold the top of the clutch down and determine where the button closure meets the leather strap overhang. Mark and punch using a 4.0 mm size hole. At the top edge of that hole, punch an additional 2.3 mm size hole that slightly overlaps the large hole to make a keyhole shape **(I)**. Secure the strap over the button closure.

4. Lightly hammer the leather along the two folds to help flatten them down, and press the wool folds of your clutch with a hot iron and a bit of steam.

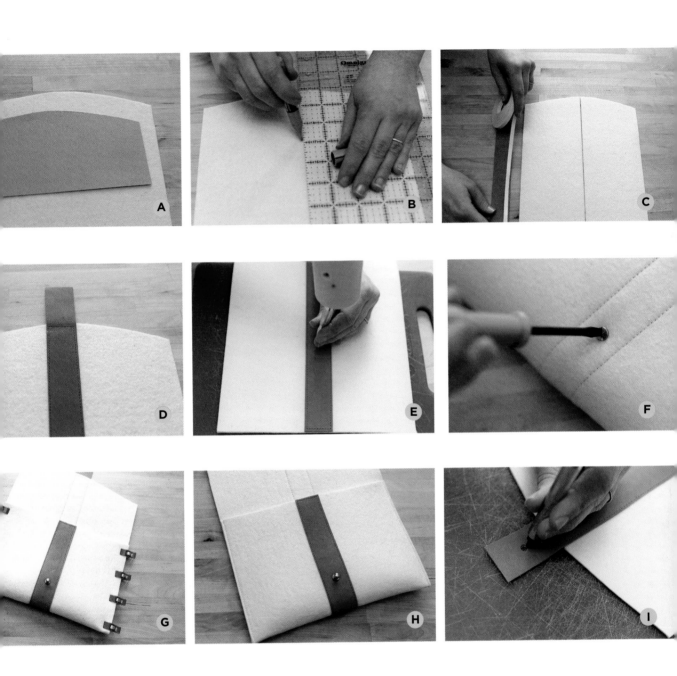

LEATHER
DOPP KIT

Let's face it — it's not always easy to give handmade goods that men like. Skip the fabric and go straight to the good stuff with this boxed toiletry bag. The leather will look better and better with each use. It's just the right size for essentials like shaving cream, a razor, and soap. You can keep the bag basic or add some personality using metal stamping.

A NOTE ON LEATHER FOR THIS PROJECT:

You want to select a piece of leather that has some structure, but that isn't too thick. There are a lot of layers in this one.

Materials

Leather: 3 oz., at least 12" x 16"

10" antique brass zipper

Wonder tape

Leather glue

Double-sided tape

Coordinating general-weight polyester thread for bobbin that matches zipper tape

Upper and bobbin thread that matches your leather

Low-tack masking tape

Zipper foot sewing machine attachment

Scissors

Acrylic ruler

Leather shears

Mallet

Metal stamps (optional)

Cutting

From leather, cut:

(2) 7" x 11" rectangles for the main exterior

(1) 1¼" x 7" rectangle for the handle

STAMPING (OPTIONAL)

The area that will be on the side of the finished bag is centered 2″ from each short side and 3″ from the top long side **(A)**.

1. Position the leather on a firm flat surface. Attach a piece of low-tack masking tape straight across the leather to act as a guide for your stamping.

2. Place the metal stamp design against the leather firmly, making sure the letter is oriented correctly **(B)**.

3. Hit the top of stamp handle with your mallet 3–5 times.

4. Continue with remaining stamps.

SEWING

1. Because leather doesn't fray, you can sew it directly onto the zipper without folding the raw edge under. Position a piece of wonder tape on the wrong side along the top long edge of your first piece of leather. Place the leather centered directly on top of the zipper tape, about $1/8$″ from the zipper teeth, wrong side down so the tape is sandwiched in between. Press with your fingers to stick them together **(C)**.

2. Using a stitch length of 3, a zipper foot and upholstery-weight thread, topstitch the leather to the zipper tape $1/8$″ from the raw edge of the leather **(D)**.

3. Repeat with the second piece of leather on the opposite side of the zipper.

4. Open the zipper $2/3$ of the way.

5. Fold the leather pieces right sides together so the bottom edges are lined up. Sew together using a $3/8$″ seam allowance. Tie off your thread ends **(E)**.

6. Open the seam and flatten it out using a mallet and glue.

7. Flatten the bag so that the bottom seam is centered and lined up with the zipper underneath. Sew across both sides using a $3/8$″ seam allowance, taking care not to sew over the metal zipper stops **(F)**.

8. At each corner mark a square 1″ from the side fold and 1″ from your stitching line **not the raw edge (G)**.

9. Hold the layers together tightly. Using leather shears, cut out your squares through the two layers of leather. Repeat on the other three corners **(H)**.

10. Beginning on the side of the bag with the closed end of the zipper, pinch the corner up to close the box, ensuring that both sides are straight and matched up. Sew together with a $1/4$″ seam allowance. Repeat on the other corner **(I)**.

11. To insert the handle, repeat Step 10 for the other side. But before stitching the sides closed, insert the leather handle so that it is tucked inside the pouch and comes out centered between the folded corners. The wrong side of the leather handle will face the right side of the main bag leather. Let $1/2$″ extend past the seam line on each side **(J)**.

12. Sew the corners together with a $1/4$″ seam allowance. You will be going through many layers of leather, so slow down and use your hand wheel.

13. Clean up thread ends by knotting, trimming and melting them (see page 95).

14. Place a piece of double-sided tape in between the side seam to flatten the zipper down. Press and lightly hammer if necessary. Repeat with the ends of the handle, securing them to the sides of the bag.

15. Turn the bag right side out and press out the corners with your finger **(K)**.

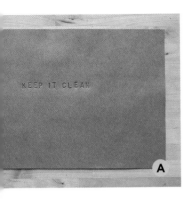

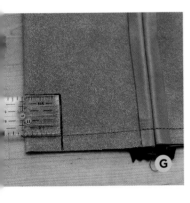

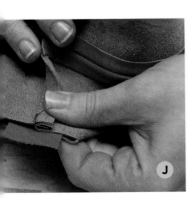

ENVELOPE BOTTOM
BAG

There is something about leather that can turn the most basic of bags into a luxury item. The folded envelope bottom on this tote looks complicated and so different from the typical boxed corners, but it is actually very simple and quick to sew. This is your opportunity to splurge on a really beautiful piece of leather.

Materials

Leather: 2–3 oz., at least 42" square

8 metal rivets

Coordinating upholstery weight thread

3.5 mm leather hole punch

Double-sided tape

Rubber mallet

Sharp scissors

Chalk pen

Leather sewing machine needle

Acrylic ruler

Cutting

From leather, cut:
(2) 12½" x 21" side panels
(1) 6½" x 42" gusset
(2) 2¼" x 24" straps
(1) 8" x 7" pocket
(1) 8" x 5½" pocket

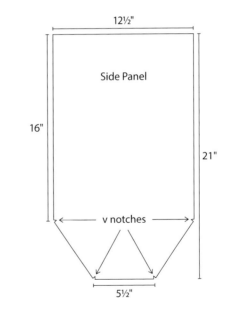

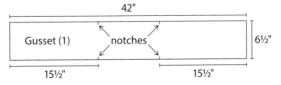

Figure 1

CUTTING

1. Referencing Figure 1, cut 4 small ¼" notches on the gusset pieces, 15½" from either end on both sides **(A)**.

2. Referencing the measurments in Figure 1, cut the angles and ¼" V notches from the sides and bottom of each side panel **(B)**. This reduces bulk when folding.

SEWING THE POCKET AND BAG

1. Place the two pocket pieces wrong sides together, aligning the bottom and sides. Stitch along the sides and bottom **(C)**. Tie off your threads (see page 95).

2. On the wrong side of the bottom three edges of each side panel adhere double-sided tape.

3. Starting with the angled sides, fold the edge ½" to the wrong side. Hammer the seams flat with your mallet.

4. Fold the bottom edge ½" to the wrong side. Hammer the seam flat **(D)**.

5. Using a chalk pen and a ruler, mark a line ½" from the side edges, on the wrong side of each panel and connect the two with another line **(E)**.

6. On the wrong side of both side panels, place double-sided tape on the 16" sides.

7. Starting at the top edge of one side panel, adhere your gusset panel right side facing the wrong side of the side panel along the tape and lining up the edge of the gusset with the chalk line **(F)**.

8. Aligning the notches, bring the gusset across the bottom of the bag **(G)**.

9. Place double-sided tape on three sides and fold over the envelope bottom. Adhere to the right side of the gusset **(H)**.

10. Adhere the remaining long edge of the gusset along the chalked line.

11. Starting at the top, edgestitch down the side of the bag, along the envelope folds, and back up the other side. Tie off threads (see page 95) **(H)**.

12. Repeat Steps 7–11 for other side panel.

MAKING THE HANDLES

1. Attach double-sided tape on the wrong sides along both long edges of the two handle pieces **(I)**.

2. Fold each leather handle piece in thirds, pressing the tape to adhere **(J)**.

3. Stitch down the center of each handle. Tie your thread ends (see page 95).

ATTACHING THE RIVETS

1. Mark the center on the short end (top) of each side panel. With the right side facing up, center the pocket on the wrong side of one side panel using the center-mark as a guide **(K)**. With a chalk pen, mark the position of the pocket on the inside of each side panel piece.

2. On the pocket, mark 1" in and ½" away from the top raw edge. Mark 1" in and ½" away from the pocket raw edge. Repeat on the other side of the pocket. Punch 4 rivet holes using a 3.5 mm leather punch.

3. Using the pocket as a template, reposition the pocket onto the center of the side panel. Mark and punch 4 holes into the side panel. Repeat for the opposite side panel.

4. On one side panel, position the straps 3" deep, between the side panel and the pocket. Using the pocket as a template, mark and punch 2 holes into each strap end.

5. Reposition the handle ends under the pocket. Align the holes, insert the rivets and hammer them in to secure **(L)**.

6. Repeat Steps 2 –5 for the opposite handle omitting the pocket.

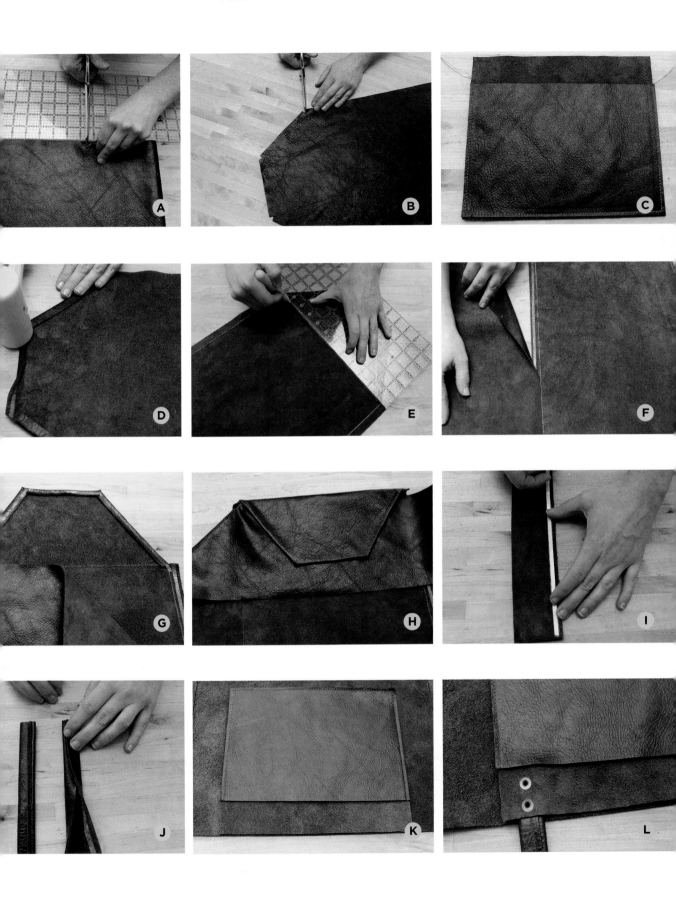

BIAS TAPE

When I began sewing, using bias tape in my projects was not on my agenda. First of all, I had no clue why I should use it, and the process of sewing it on seemed really confusing. I thought the prepackaged polyester stuff from the fabric store felt icky and didn't come in enough of the colors I would want to use. Well, guess what? It's not that hard to make! It doesn't take much fabric to get a whole lot of tape. And it's pretty easy (and fun!) to sew with.

MAKING YOUR OWN BIAS TAPE

I am including this method for making bias tape because it's simple and easy to understand. If you still hate making it, look for premade bias tape from beautiful fabrics (hello, Nani Iro and Liberty of London!) on etsy and other internet shops.

Materials

Fabric: ½ yard

Cutting mat

Acrylic ruler (at least 12″ in length)

Rotary cutter

Matching thread

Bias tape maker (see chart on page 134 for size options)

CUTTING INSTRUCTIONS

1. Cut a 15″ square of fabric.

2. Fold the square, wrong sides together to form a triangle.

3. Place the folded triangle on your cutting mat so that the fold is closest to your body and lined up **(A)**.

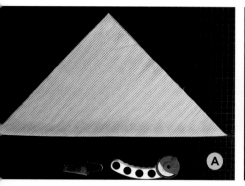

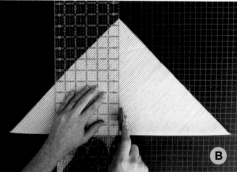

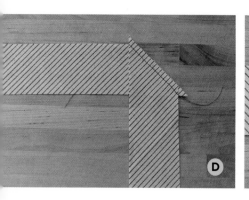

4. Cut a perpendicular line from the top point of the triangle down to the fold. You will now have two triangles **(B)**.

5. Beginning at the long cut edge on one triangle, cut strips the width determined by your project. When you get about 4″ from the corner, stop cutting strips (they start to get too short at that point). Repeat for the other triangle **(C)**.

JOINING BIAS STRIPS

1. Each of your strips will have ends cut at a 45-degree angle. You will sew together opposite ends of these strips using a ¼″ seam allowance .

> **TIP:** If you get confused at the beginning about matching up opposite ends, test it first. Join the two strips together with your fingers where you will sew them together, and flip the top strip right side up. If it lines up with the other strip, you're good! If it forms a V shape, you need to use the other end of your top strip.

2. Take your first strip and position it right side up on your sewing machine bed. Take a second strip and position it right side down so that the angles align **(D)**.

3. Make sure those little "ears" are there with ¼″ from the intersection to the edge of the strip to allow for the seam.

4. Sew together using a ¼″ seam allowance. Press your seam open. Clip off the ears **(E)**.

5. Continue adding on strips until you use them all, alternating longer and shorter lengths to space out the seams. To save time, join all of your strips before pressing the seams.

BIAS TAPE MAKER

I highly recommend using a nifty tool called a bias tape maker to add to your sewing room bag of tricks. The bias tape width will be more consistent, and you'll save both your fingers and your sanity.

SINGLE FOLD VS. DOUBLE FOLD

Single fold bias tape is what will come directly out of your bias tape maker. This means that the two raw edges are folded in and pressed to the middle of your strip. This is what you will use for bias tape appliqué because it is less bulky than the double fold.

Double fold bias tape is single fold bias tape, folded in half down the length of the tape and pressed again. It makes a little mouth to sandwich an edge of fabric inside. This is what you will use for bindings and fabric ties.

USING A BIAS TAPE MAKER

Bias tape makers come in a range of sizes: 6 mm ($\frac{1}{4}$"), 12 mm ($\frac{1}{2}$"), 18 mm ($\frac{3}{4}$"), 25 mm (1"), and 50 mm (2"). The measurement you see on the package is the finished width of single fold bias tape that it makes, and twice the finished width of double fold bias tape. For example, if you want to make $\frac{1}{2}$" single fold bias tape for appliqué, you need a 12 mm bias tape maker. If you want $\frac{1}{2}$" double fold bias tape, you need a 25 mm bias tape maker.

BIAS TAPE MAKER SIZE	WIDTH TO CUT YOUR BIAS STRIPS	FINISHED SINGLE FOLD WIDTH	FINISHED DOUBLE FOLD WIDTH
6 mm ($\frac{1}{4}$")	$\frac{1}{2}$"	$\frac{1}{4}$"	$\frac{1}{8}$"
12 mm ($\frac{1}{2}$")	1"	$\frac{1}{2}$"	$\frac{1}{4}$"
18 mm ($\frac{3}{4}$")	$1\frac{1}{2}$"	$\frac{3}{4}$"	$\frac{3}{8}$"
25 mm (1")	2"	1"	$\frac{1}{2}$"
50 mm (2")	4"	2"	1"

1. Feed the angled end of your assembled bias strip wrong side up into the U-shaped opening, making sure that your fabric is centered and not twisted. Insert a pin or the end of your seam ripper down the channel to help scoot your strip out of the narrow end of the bias tape maker. The strip will start to come out with the raw edges folded to the center **(A)**.

2. Hold the handle of the bias tape maker with one hand, and place a very hot iron on top of the bias tape right next to the opening. Simultaneously, with your other hand, pull the bias tape maker back along your ironing board so that the bias tape continues to come out of the narrow end, and you are pressing it flat as you pull **(B)**. Continue until you get to the end of the strip.

TIP: Do not use a steam setting when ironing your bias tape! You will be holding the handle of the bias tape maker just a few inches from the head of the iron and risk a serious steam scald. Instead, put your iron on the hottest setting and press your bias tape with steam later if necessary.

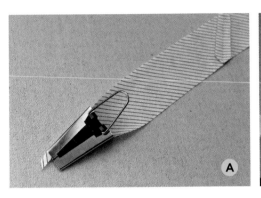

TROUBLESHOOTING

Are the edges of your tape wobbly and the edges hard to center? Is your fabric thinner than average quilting cotton? You might need to cut your strip just slightly larger with thin fabrics such as shot cotton, lawn, or voile. When I use lighter weight fabrics, I cut my strips $1/8''$ wider than usual. So for making $1/2''$ single fold bias tape, I will cut my strips to $1 1/8''$ instead of $1''$.

BANG FOR YOUR BUCK

So how much bias tape do you get from a 15″ square of fabric?

When you cut 1″ strips for a $1/2''$ single fold bias tape such as we'll use in the Tree Rings quilt, you'll get 200″ of bias tape!

When you cut 2″ strips for a $1/2''$ double fold bias binding that we'll use in the apron project, you'll get 112″ of tape!

That's a lot of bias tape for not a whole lot of fabric.

SEWING WITH BIAS TAPE

BIAS TAPE AS BINDING

The process of binding encloses the raw edges of a project and can also add a decorative touch. This method is most commonly used around the outer edges of quilts but can be used to add decorative details to garments too.

There are two ways to sew double fold bias tape on as a binding.

1. Unfold your bias tape. Place it on the back side of your project right sides together so the raw edge of the bias tape lines up with the raw edge of your project. Pin **(A)**.

Begin your stitching line at least 6″ past the end of your bias tape (this will help you join together the ends later). Sew just inside the first crease of the binding, continuing until you are about

8″ from where you started. Join the ends together as noted below. Finish attaching the bias binding. Fold the binding to the other side of your project. Attach by machine- or by hand-sewing **(B)**.

2. You can also sandwich the bias tape over a raw edge so it's enclosed, pin, and then edgestitch the tape through all the layers. In theory, this works, but I find that I am always bound to miss spots on the back side. I also don't enjoy the time it takes to do the pinning.

JOINING BIAS TAPE ENDS

Joining two ends of bias tape (or straight grain binding) is easy! I had always used a really cool binding tool, but I forgot it on a quilting retreat. There I learned that the secret formula wasn't such a secret.

1. Measure the width of your unfolded bias tape. Subtract ¼″. This will be the measurement you will use to determine the necessary overlap of your two bias tape ends.

> ### WIDTH OF UNFOLDED BIAS TAPE (OR BINDING) - ¼″ = LENGTH OF OVERLAP

So, for a ½″ double fold bias binding that measures 2″ wide total, you will trim your binding so that the edges overlap 1¾″.

2. Position the ends right sides together at a 90-degree angle **(C)**.

3. Stitch diagonally from corner to corner. Trim the seam allowance to ¼″ and press the seam open **(D)**.

SINGLE FOLD BIAS TAPE

To attach single fold bias tape as an appliqué, first secure the tape to the base fabric with some wonder tape. Then edgestitch along the edges — or, if you are more patient than I am, attach by hand.

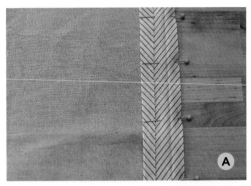

TREE RINGS
BIAS TAPE QUILT

Bias tape is such a great material. Don't just relegate it to binding. In this quilt, I used bias tape much like I would a marker, appliquéing it on to create a modern design straight out of my sketchbook. It's really easy to adjust the sizes of the rings too — just do the math! I used single fold bias tape to make the design, and double fold bias tape to bind the finished quilt.

Finished Size:
42" x 56"

Materials

Background: 1³⁄₄ yards of 44"-wide fabric

Backing: 2³⁄₄ yards of 44"-wide fabric

Ring fabric: 1 fat quarter (18" x 22") each of Fabrics A, B, C, D and E

Binding: ½ yard

Batting: 48" x 60"

Wonder Tape

Iron

Coordinating threads for ring fabrics

Masking tape

Basting pins

Spray baste (optional)

Cutting

From the background fabric, cut:
(1) 43" x 56" rectangle

From each of the ring fabrics, cut:
(1) 15" square from Fabrics A, B, C, D and E

From the binding fabric, cut:
(2) 18" squares

MAKING BIAS TAPE

1. Referencing page 132, make ½" single fold bias tape out of each of the ring fabrics, and ½" double fold bias tape out of the binding fabric.

2. Cut the following lengths of each single fold bias tape:

Ring 1 (Fabric A): 23"
Ring 2 (Fabric B): 36"
Ring 3 (Fabric C): 48"
Ring 4 (Fabric D): 61"
Ring 5 (Fabric E): 73"
Ring 6 (Fabric B): 85"
Ring 7 (Fabric A): 97"

3. Join the ends of each single fold bias tape to make a total of 7 rings. Make sure the tape is not twisted before you sew **(A)**.

> **MATH LESSON:** It's easy to find out how much bias tape you'll need to create a certain size circle!
>
> Diameter of the Circle x 3.14 = Circumference
>
> Length to Cut the Bias Tape = Circumference + ¾" (for the overlap joining the ends)
>
> In this case, where ¼" doesn't matter so much, I just added 1" instead of ¾" for the overlap.

ATTACHING THE RINGS

1. Fold your background fabric in half lengthwise, then in half again in the other direction. Press the folds. This marks the center of the quilt top and makes it easier to arrange the rings.

2. Press each fabric ring flat, curving it on your ironing board to start molding it into a flat circle **(B)**.

3. Start with Ring A (the smallest) and apply wonder tape to the wrong side. It's helpful to hold the ring of fabric in your hand and let it hang as you attach the tape **(C)**.

4. Arrange the ring on your background fabric, using the center crease marks to center it. Press with your fingers to secure the tape, then iron it down.

5. Attach the ring to the quilt by edgestitching along both edges of the bias strip **(D)**. Pull your beginning and ending threads to the back and tie them off.

6. Repeat Steps 3–5 with the remaining rings.

> **ARE YOU HAVING A HARD TIME MAKING THE RINGS EVEN ON EACH SIDE?**
> Before you add on the wonder tape, fold the bias tape into fourths. Press the folds lightly with your iron to mark the quarters. You can line up these creases with the creases on your background fabric.

QUILTING

1. Lay your backing fabric right side down on the floor. Secure it to the floor with masking tape, pulling the fabric taut.

2. Place your batting on top of the backing fabric and smooth it out.

3. Place your quilt top right side up on top of the batting. Baste with pins or spray baste.

4. Quilt as desired. I like to echo the rings in the negative space between **(D, E)**.

> **TIP:** If quilt making is new to you, check out the free Quilt Making Basics download at www.luckyspool.com.

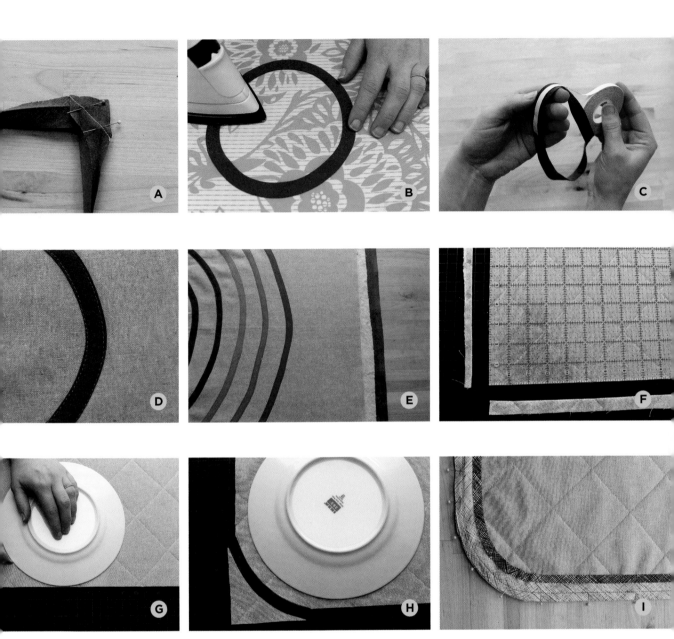

BINDING

1. Trim the quilt so its edges are square **(F)**.

2. Trace a dinner plate over the curve on each corner of the quilt. Trim each corner along this line to get rounded corners **(G, H)**.

3. Apply the double fold bias binding to the front of the quilt (see page 136). Hand-sew to the back **(I)**.

BIAS TAPE BOUND APRON WITH LEATHER POCKET

A good apron is a necessity when you are working with inks and dyes. Just because you might use it to wipe your hands on or catch stray splatters doesn't mean it needs to be basic. Begin by using a dyed canvas, bind it with some fantastic double fold bias tape, and attach a great leather pocket. This apron won't take long to make, so you'll have more time for other projects!

Materials

6 oz. or 8 oz. PFD 60"-wide canvas: 1¼ yard

½" double fold bias tape: 3 yards

1" natural cotton twill tape: 3 yards

Leather: 2 oz., 6" x 8"

(4) ¼" eyelets

(4) small (¼") metal rivets

3.5 mm leather hole punch

Dyeing supplies (see page 74)

Leather sewing machine needle

Coordinating upholstery-weight polyester thread

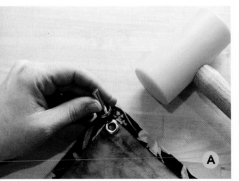
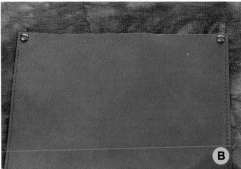

DYEING THE CANVAS

1. Prewash your canvas in hot water and synthrapol. This will prepare it for dyeing and take care of any shrinkage before you cut your apron pieces.

2. Dye your canvas (see page 76). Wash, dry, and press.

CUTTING

1. Fold dyed canvas in half vertically. Trace the Underarm Curve and Bottom Curve templates (see page 157) and position at the top and bottom of the canvas aligning the edges of the pattern along the fold. Cut out the main apron.

2. From the twill tape, cut: (1) 24" length for the neck tie and (2) 40" lengths for the waist ties.

ASSEMBLING

1. Bind the raw edges of your apron with bias tape (see page 136).

2. Referencing Figure 1 for placement, attach 4 eyelets (see page 97) at the top and side corners of the apron as indicated **(A)**.

3. Place the leather pocket so that the top edge is 15" from the top raw edge of the apron and centered along the width of the apron. Sew the sides and bottom of the leather pocket to the apron, backstitching on the canvas at each end.

4. Punch a hole at each corner of the leather pocket using your 3.5 mm punch. Secure each corner of the pocket with rivets (see page 96) **(B)**.

5. Knot one end of each twill tape waist tie. Slip them through the eyelets at the side of the apron from front to back **(C)**.

6. Run the twill tape neck tie through the eyelets at the top of the apron from back to front. Knot each end.

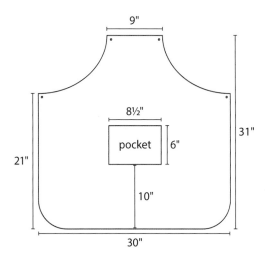

Figure 1

TEMPLATES & ARTWORK

**SUPER HASHTAG
BLOCK PRINTED SCARF**

LEATHER BOTTOM ZIPPERED POUCH

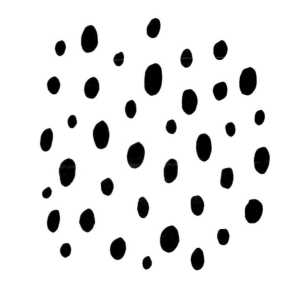

SPRING FIELD BLOCK PRINTED TEA TOWEL

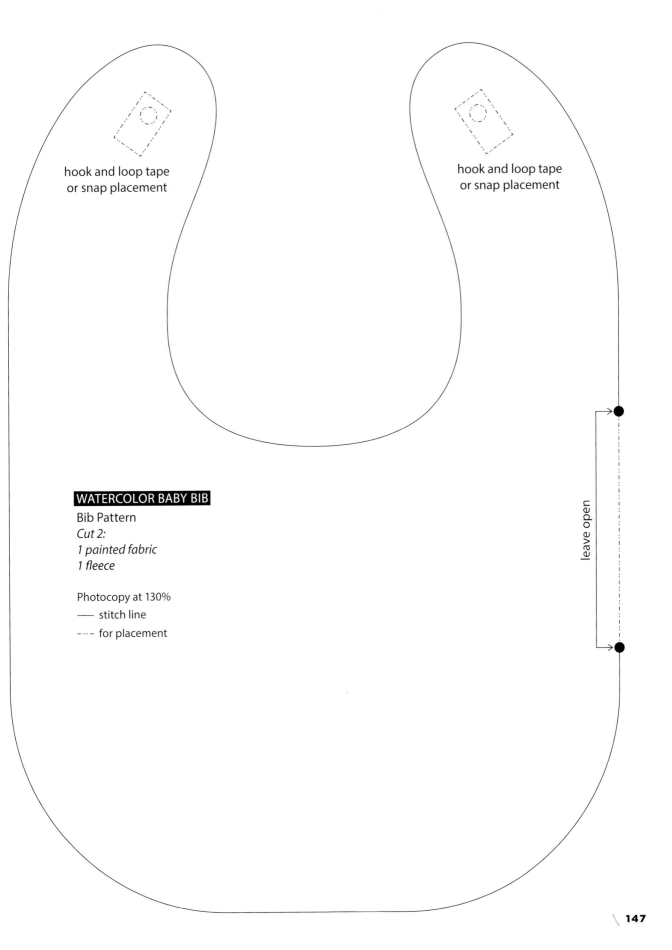

hook and loop tape
or snap placement

hook and loop tape
or snap placement

leave open

WATERCOLOR BABY BIB

Bib Pattern
Cut 2:
1 painted fabric
1 fleece

Photocopy at 130%

—— stitch line

---- for placement

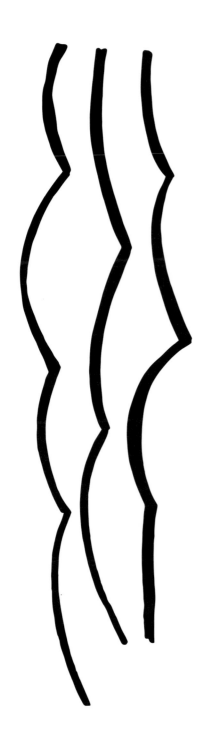

Enlarge 125%

**NATURE'S ABSTRACT
SCREEN PRINTED
CANVAS (SCREEN 2)**

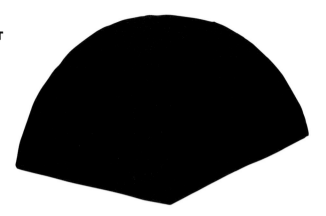

Enlarge 125%

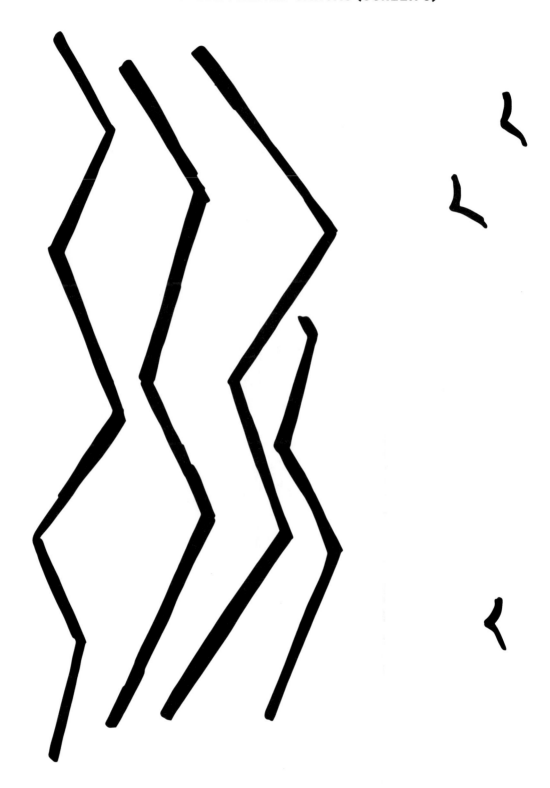

Enlarge 125%

**BEST FRIENDS
STUFFIES
(BUNNY)**

Enlarge 140%

LEATHER HEXAGON PILLOW
Hexagon Template
Cut 8 from leather
Actual Size

LEATHER BRACELET
Stitching Template

Actual Size

PAINTED LEATHER BASKET

Small, Medium and Large Basket Pattern
Cut 1:
1 painted leather

Small: Actual Size
Medium: Enlarge 133%
Large: Enlarge 167%

LEATHER WRAPPED WOOL CLUTCH
Curved Template

Actual Size

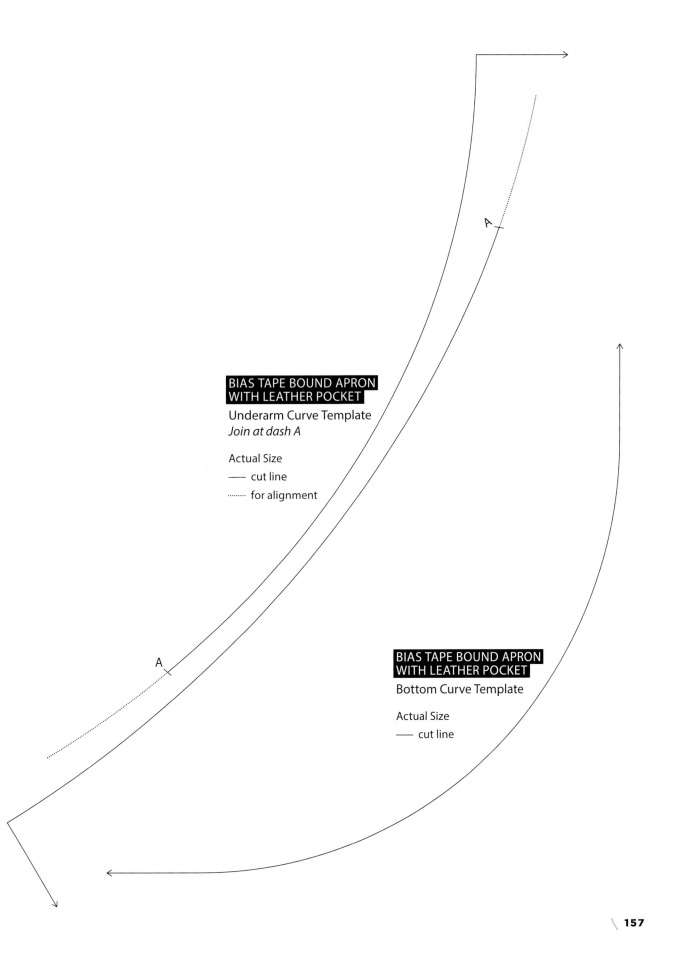

BIAS TAPE BOUND APRON WITH LEATHER POCKET

Underarm Curve Template
Join at dash A

Actual Size
—— cut line
········ for alignment

BIAS TAPE BOUND APRON WITH LEATHER POCKET

Bottom Curve Template

Actual Size
—— cut line

A

A

RESOURCES

DHARMA TRADING CO.
www.dharmatrading.com
Fabric dye supplies
Fabric paints and dyes
Leather paints
Prepared-for-dye fabrics

DICK BLICK ART MATERIALS
www.dickblick.com
Screen printing supplies: screens,
squeegees, inks, chemicals
Block printing supplies: rubber blocks, ink
Fabric dye supplies
Fabric paints and dyes
Sketchbooks and pens

ETSY
www.etsy.com
Fabric, hardware, and premade bias tape

LEE VALLEY TOOLS
www.leevalley.com
Rotary cutter and blades

OAKSHOTT FABRICS
www.oakshottfabrics.com
High-quality shot cotton fabrics

ORGANIC COTTON PLUS
www.organiccottonplus.com
Organic, ready-to-dye fabrics

THE SNAP SOURCE
www.snapsource.com
SnapSetters and quality snaps in all sizes
and colors

TANDY LEATHER FACTORY
www.tandyleatherfactory.com
Leather, punches, dyes, and findings

ZIPIT ZIPPERS
www.etsy.com/shop/zipit
Zippers in every size and color
imaginable!

Dedication

For my husband, Rob, who makes it possible for me to follow my dreams. He taught me to value my hobbies, gave me my first very own sewing machine, and respects that my need to create is an important part of who I am. And for my children, Avery, Claire, Cooper, and Charlotte, who inspire me every day with their own creativity, musical talents, and ideas.

Acknowledgments

Thank you again to my family, who supported me and believed in me long before I began writing this book. A big thank-you to my mom, Karen Roe; my mother-in-law, Rita Fleckenstein; and my good friend Bridget McBride for helping me with mom duties so I would have time to commit to this book. Thank you to Susanne Woods for convincing me that I had something special to share. My book would just be a jumble of words without the creative talents of Paula Pepin, Holly DeGroot, Kari Vojtechovsky, Shea Henderson, Lisa Lester, and Rae Ann Spitzenberger. Thank you for making this book so beautiful! Thank you to Lizzy House, for helping rekindle my love of printing. Thank you to my fellow Kristas, Krista Hennebury and Krista Withers, for being two of the most inspiring friends anyone could hope to sew (and share a name) with. And lastly, for all of my friends near and far who have been my cheerleaders throughout my years of making: I couldn't have done it without you.